PAINT LIKE
RENOIR

UNLOCK THE SECRETS OF
THE MASTER OF IMPRESSIONISM

PAINT LIKE
RENOIR

UNLOCK THE SECRETS OF
THE MASTER OF IMPRESSIONISM

Damian Callan

PAINT LIKE RENOIR

First published in the United Kingdom in 2014 by
ILEX
210 High Street
Lewes
East Sussex
BN7 2NS

Distributed worldwide (except North America)
by Thames & Hudson Ltd., 181A High Holborn,
London WC1V 7QX, United Kingdom

PUBLISHER: Alastair Campbell
EXECUTIVE PUBLISHER: Roly Allen
COMMISSIONING EDITOR: Zara Larcombe
EDITORIAL DIRECTOR: Nick Jones
SENIOR PROJECT EDITOR: Natalia Price-Cabrera
SENIOR SPECIALIST EDITOR: Frank Gallaugher
ASSISTANT EDITOR: Rachel Silverlight
ART DIRECTOR: Julie Weir
DESIGNER: Lisa McCormick
IN-HOUSE DESIGNER: Kate Haynes

British Library Cataloguing-in-Publication Data
A catalogue record for this book is available from
the British Library.

ISBN: 978-1-78157-248-1

Colour Origination by Ivy Press Reprographics

Printed and bound in China

10 9 8 7 6 5 4 3 2 1

CONTENTS

INTRODUCTION 6

CHAPTER 1

SETTING UP YOUR STUDIO 10
Materials 12
Studio & Equipment 14
Subject Matter 16
Plein Air *Studio* 18

CHAPTER 2

RENOIR CLOSE UP 20
Landscape & Impressionism 22
Portraits & Figure Groups 26
Still Life 30
Nudes 32

CHAPTER 3

PLEIN AIR RENOIR 34
Selecting a Composition 36
Starting the Composition 38
Developing the Painting 40
Masterclass: Arran from Skipness 42
Brush Technique & Detail 44
Masterclass: Daffodils & View Through Trees 48
Exercises 52

CHAPTER 4

PORTRAITS 54
Brush Technique: Two Stages 56
Masterclass: Girl Reading in Window Seat 60
Masterclass: Portrait of a Boy 64
Individual Features 68
Masterclass: Portrait of a Girl 72
Exercises 76

CHAPTER 5

FIGURE GROUPS 78
Approaching the Composition 80
Masterclass: Two Girls in the Garden 84
Masterclass: Dappled Light 86
Masterclass: Figures on a Bench 90
Exercises 92

CHAPTER 6

RENOIR & STILL LIFE 94
Experiments in Still Life 96
Masterclass: Flowers in a Vase 98
Masterclass: Yellow Roses 100
Alla Prima & Still Life 102
Masterclass: Bottle & Glass 106
Exercise 108

CHAPTER 7

RENOIR'S NUDES 110
Glazing 112
Scumbling 114
Alla Prima 116
Masterclass: Bathing Nude 118
Exercises 122

Glossary 124
Index 126
Acknowledgments & Picture Credits 128

INTRODUCTION

Pierre-Auguste Renoir was a founding member of the Impressionist movement and is one of the most popular artists of the modern era. His initial career as a painter of porcelain probably influenced the very particular way in which he handled the medium of oil paint. He met Édouard Manet, Edgar Degas and Alfred Sisley at Charles Gleyre's atelier in Paris, where they had all gone to gain a more modern and vital training in painting than the old-fashioned, rather stuffy academies could offer. He also met Claude Monet there, and together they painted side by side outdoors and established the new Impressionist way of seeing and recording the world in daylight. He went on to develop various themes, generally featuring people—often his friends—as crowds, parties, bathing nudes and portraits; as well as still lifes of flowers and fruit.

Impressionism was a revolution in painting, and to get a true sense of its impact it is well worth visiting the Musée d'Orsay on the banks of the Seine in Paris. Making your way through the dark lower floors, with their paintings from the eighteenth and early nineteenth centuries, you ascend to the top floor where you emerge into a beautifully lit space, with skylights above and doors that open out to balconies overlooking the river. All around you the walls are covered with Impressionist paintings, each one bursting with light and life. For those wishing to learn to use oil paint in a lively and individual way, the Impressionists make ideal teachers. The paint they used is not so different from products available today—as opposed to the somewhat mysterious methods of the Old Masters, grinding and mixing their pigments according to long-lost recipes—and each of them handled the medium in a personal way.

Oil paint has tremendous versatility. From a diluted and transparent glaze or scumble through to a thick impasto mark, Renoir employed the whole range of its possible applications, often within the same painting; and this is one of the most valuable reasons for studying his work. To some extent Renoir is a painter's painter: an artist whose experiments and investigations in oil paint have opened the door to new approaches by the artists who followed him. His paintings were usually begun on a plain white canvas, onto which bright colors were rubbed and smudged in. The image evolved gradually as the layers were built up—darks were kept thin, and lighter areas treated with more solid paint. The transparency of Renoir's colors heightens their intensity and contributes a jewel-like quality to some of his paintings. In other parts of a Renoir painting you find the opaque Impressionist *"tache"*—marks placed side by side creating an animated and colorful surface. Here and there you can also identify *alla prima*, or "wet-on-wet" oil painting, showing a spontaneous, gestural response to his subject. Already you can see there are a panoply of painting techniques to learn from. Studying and imitating Renoir, you will learn to enjoy both the feel of the paint and the surprises turned up by the process of applying layers.

You will learn how to build up a painting in thin layers of diluted paint, by first establishing the dark values and half-tones, then going on to strengthen the lighter areas with fine trails of thicker paint. In this way the painting emerges gradually and organically, often presenting the artist with surprises or "happy accidents." The sense of discovery this way of working entails is a tremendous gift to the artistic process. Renoir seems to encompass the entire range of the history of Western painting—from the luminous glazes of the Old Masters' through to the Impressionists' impasto mark—in his works. Renoir claimed he saw "one thousand tints" and appeared to paint (some of) them with a tiny brush—the influence of his early training with porcelain, no doubt.

The practical element of this book begins with an introduction to the Impressionist approach to painting outdoors, focusing on Renoir's particular responses to the effects of daylight on his subjects and his instinctive use of color. We then go on to look at his studio work and choice of subject matter. Renoir was, above all, a figure painter and he stressed his need to be among people, so we will examine his approaches to figure painting in some depth, as well as the basics of the art of portraiture and how Renoir dealt specifically with this form. We will also examine some of the ways in which he combined several figures and groups of figures in more complex compositions. At times, Renoir rested while painting still-life subjects. In these moments, he would experiment more freely with technique and paint handling inspired by the forms and textures of fruit and flowers. Sometimes he appeared to push his work with oils into an almost sculptural, tactile approach, painting not just what he saw but also what he knew of the feel of the textures and forms of the objects before him. Renoir loved to depict lively and life-filled subjects. His philosophy was a positive one and he consciously chose life-affirming subject matter. "There are enough ugly things in life for us not to add to them," he said.

Each of the different subject areas and the techniques Renoir used will be explored and broken down into clear stages. Many sections are accompanied by a step-by-step Masterclass, in which the development of a particular image is clearly demonstrated. At the end of each chapter you will find exercises that offer simple, practical ways to develop your own work, following the subject of that particular chapter. By exploring Renoir's various approaches you should gain an appetite for entering into a process with oil paint, enjoying the freedom and spontaneity of applying paint without the use of outlines and finding your subject gradually as color relationships begin to develop, leading you on a path of discovery.

Before illustrating and emulating Renoir's many approaches to his different themes, we will look closely at examples of his own work and attempt to analyze and articulate some of his distinctive methods and artistic concerns. The points made about how these images were brought to their conclusions will be repeated and revisited in each of the chapters, which will endeavor to emulate the master's technique. First, however, we will set out some of the kinds of materials and equipment required to begin your exploration of Renoir's technique.

CHAPTER 1: SETTING UP YOUR STUDIO

Renoir practiced his craft both in the studio and *en plein air*. Developing his particular style alongside Claude Monet in the outdoor environment, Renoir took a lot from the experience of being there in the changing moment—an experience that was quite different from the still, artificial environment of working in a studio. He typically worked from life—but as this is not always possible we will also look at the best ways of using photographs and drawings for your compositions.

Before we come to the practical considerations, however, this chapter first sets out the basic materials required for attempting to paint in the manner of Renoir, and guidance is offered on the different sorts of materials available and how you might determine which kind to choose. You will find the materials outlined here mentioned in the Masterclass and Exercise sections of the coming chapters, but you may find it useful to refer back to the fuller descriptions and explanations offered here when making your preparations to work.

As well as materials, you will also find advice on organizing your workspace; how you might equip it and arrange it, whether you have a dedicated studio space to work in or just a stolen corner of your home. Further advice is offered on working outdoors in front of your landscape subject.

SETTING UP YOUR STUDIO
Materials

CANVAS

Renoir appears to have painted exclusively on canvas, and the stages by which he built up layers of oil paint rely on the ability of this surface to both absorb thinned paint into its weave and carry thicker paint on the top of the threads. For quick experiments and studies it's a good idea use pre-primed canvas bought on a roll, which can be cut to size and stuck to a board for working on—just as you might do with paper for pastel or drawing work. Larger pieces are best done on unprimed canvas, stretched on wooden stretchers and then primed with two or three coats of gesso—but this is a long, laborious process best saved for a point when you are experienced in handling oil paint and have some clear ideas about the particular piece of work you hope to produce. Until then, you may want to save yourself time and effort by buying ready-stretched canvases, which should also make you less inhibited about experimenting. The quality of a canvas will be reflected in its price, but cheaper products will do while you are building up your confidence and experience.

In general, Renoir liked a fine grade of canvas and a white primer—his first layer of diluted paints appeared particularly luminous on this bright surface. On occasion he would use a pale, tinted ground such as red-brown or beige.

It is recommended that to begin with you work fairly small so that you can develop your paintings quickly—and will therefore get more experience of working through the various stages that are outlined in this book.

OIL PAINTS

These are available in student quality or artists' quality. The former are cheaper and inferior in quality but, as the name suggests, they are intended for the apprentice and perfectly acceptable to use when you are learning.

A selection similar to what Renoir would have used might include: flake white, chrome yellow, Naples yellow, yellow ocher, raw sienna, vermillion, madder red (alizarin crimson), viridian, Veronese green, cobalt blue, utramarine and ivory black. Renoir's use of black as a color came later in his career, introduced after his time in Italy, when he pronounced it the "Queen of Colors."

The preparation of your palette of mixed colors is essential. You will need some stocks of the main colors you're working with—perhaps divided into a darker and a lighter version of each color—that can be reached for without the interruption of having to stop and mix. This means that a painting can be begun in a general way and, once established, the colors can be returned to and either used again or modified and remixed as the painting develops.

Oil paint pigments will vary in opacity. Different levels of opacity will be needed for different applications—for example, a transparent pigment will be needed in the early stages of the painting or for a glaze. The opacity is usually indicated on the label of the pigment.

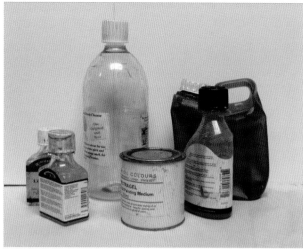

BRUSHES & PALETTE KNIVES

For handling quantities of dry oil paint, stiff hog hair brushes are best—they can pick up and deposit a dollop of paint in a direct and expressive way. They come in different shapes and sizes; I recommend square, long-handled brushes in sizes 2, 4, 6, 8, 10 and 12. Following the Impressionist approach, the size of brush relates to the size of a mark, so particular brushes may be used specifically for different parts of a painting; large sizes for the foreground, smaller for the background. The use of a long-handled brush held at its very end may be particularly helpful when attempting to emulate Renoir's approach. Not only will this technique achieve a much looser, more suggestive kind of mark, but the fact that the long handle forces you to work a reasonable distance from the image means you're effectively painting from the perspective of the viewer—the effect that the Impressionists sought, with colors and marks mixing optically, works best from a distance, where they retain their strength and intensity.

Your dedicated artists' brushes can be supplemented with larger house-painting brushes for even bigger marks. Brushes will wear out, especially when you're working on canvas, so be prepared to buy new ones. It is said that Renoir only used two or three brushes at a time and would destroy them once they wore out, just in case he should pick up the wrong one by mistake.

Renoir seemed to use mainly stiff-haired brushes (his preference was for brushes of gray marten fur made in Russia, known as Meloncillo brushes) for both the initial transparent phase of the painting as well as the later thick and opaque stages. For diluted, fluid paint, soft brushes are useful, and there are points in Renoir's work—particularly in the painting of faces and features—where he has obviously used a soft sable brush to paint both fine translucent lines as well as thicker, more solid lines around eyes and mouths.

Palette knives are also essential to the mixing of colors and the preparation of the palette. They come in trowel or butter knife shapes—use whichever helps you mix quickly.

OIL/TURPS/MEDIA

In the oil painting techniques described later in the book, you will find it is recommended that you add linseed oil to your paint to increase its fluidity and its transparency; it will also slow the drying of the paint. Turpentine, or turps, is traditionally used to thin oil paint and to clean brushes. Many artists start their paintings with a fluid product made from paint diluted with one part linseed oil to two parts turps—by the end of the painting this ratio will have increased to 1:1. Renoir had a double dipper on his palette: one part contained a mixture of equal quantities of linseed oil and turps; the other, linseed oil alone.

Like the other Impressionists, Renoir experimented with creating different paint qualities by mixing the paint with various other media. Poppy-seed oil had been adopted by some painters because of its resistance to yellowing with age; the Impressionists used it because it also made the paint thicker, and made it easier to build up textured and impasto marks. Synthetic products are now available that do a similar job—some both thickening the paint and accelerating its drying time.

SETTING UP YOUR STUDIO
Studio & Equipment

PALETTE

It is important to have a decent-sized surface on which to mix your paints so that you will be sure to mix enough paint to work with. Some artists use a sheet of glass laid over a white surface for their fixed palette, or a piece of white Formica. These can be easily cleaned of mixtures at the end of each session. It is worth mounting the large palette onto a wheeled piece of furniture, if you can find something suitable, so that you can move it easily from one working area to another. You might also have a smaller, hand-held wooden palette onto which mixtures can be transferred for working close to the painting (below left).

EASEL

Some artists prefer to work directly onto a wall—I like to take pieces of work on and off the easel and work on a number of pieces during the course of a day (below right). Unfortunately, an easel does take up a lot of room, which can limit your options if you don't have a dedicated workspace. However you choose to work, what is essential is that you are able to stand well back during the course of your painting in order to see clearly—perhaps even a little more objectively— exactly what you have just done, and adjust as necessary.

In his later years, paralyzed by arthritis, Renoir worked on an easel that incorporated a roller system, which enabled him to roll the part of the canvas on which he wanted to work to within his reach as he sat painting in his wheelchair.

STUDIO SPACE

It is great if you have a dedicated studio space where you can set work up and leave things in progress (above left). Oil paints are messy and sometimes smelly, and if you have to tidy things away at the end of each session you may find that it becomes harder and harder to ever get started again. Work left in progress, especially when left with the intention of reflecting on the next course of action, can easily be taken up again and quickly resolved—provided it is there waiting patiently for the artist to be ready. An ideal studio might have a plan chest with large, shallow drawers for storing canvases and finished work; good, consistent natural light; room to stand well back from your work and walls to display your work on. The *plein air* artist will of course also practice putting together an impromptu outdoors studio—but this will be covered shortly, in more depth.

In his later years, Renoir achieved an ideal balance between working outdoors in front of his subject and the concentrated environment of the indoor studio, by having himself built an outdoor studio—a glassed building with curtains that could be drawn across different sides in order to control the direction of the light.

DISPLAYING WORK

One of the most important benefits of having a dedicated workspace is the possibility of displaying your work while you are deciding what to do to it next (above right and below). A crucial element in the artistic process is that stage when you do nothing, pausing to consider what course of action to take next. Renoir is quoted as having said, "You have to stop work and take a stroll once in a while." Often, it is time spent looking and considering, without taking action, that helps solve many painting decisions. Renoir advocated finishing *plein air* paintings back in the studio. The quality of light and space can have a profound effect on the look and feel of a painting; it makes sense to resolve your paintings in an environment closer to the one they will eventually hang in.

Renoir learnt his brand of Impressionism out of doors, by the riverside, where he painted what he observed. His preference, however, was for figurative subjects with the occasional still life to "rest his eyes." Whether you are painting a figure, a landscape or a still life, each form comes with its own concerns—how long can you keep a fruit bowl looking fresh (and uneaten)? How do you work with something that changes as rapidly as a landscape? Often the solution is simply to work quickly, but there are other things you can do to make the process easier.

WORKING FROM LIFE: MODELS

Renoir's models were typically his friends and family who were obliged to sit and stand for poses. Sometimes they were there for most of the painting, while at other times he worked from memory or engaged models for specific parts of a larger composition. He preferred his models not to pose too stiffly

but to stay in the general position he had in mind, and from time to time, when he was ready for a particular observation or detail, he would request that they stay completely still.

Your model will need a warm, private space in which to pose. They may need their own heater, especially if they are nude. You will need good directional lighting: simple spotlights that can be clipped onto a surface/wall/ceiling are very useful. Otherwise, it may be possible to position your model near a window so that there can be a clear light source. Sometimes it is helpful to have a podium or a box for your model to stand on. Depending on your particular theme, props and pieces of furniture such as benches and stools can be useful. To a certain extent, you and your model are engaged in a game of roleplay or theater, so be creative about how you set the scene, and what you don't have to hand you can simply make up. Many of Renoir's nudes were bathers, often painted from models

seated on imaginary rocks, and the background added later from a landscape or from his imagination—a scene can be contrived with a few simple artifices. His portrait subjects often held props or were engaged in everyday activities such as reading, writing or playing with toys.

WORKING FROM LIFE: STILL LIFES

Renoir was a traditionalist in his choice of subject for still-life painting, mostly working with fruit and flowers. When working with organic matter, the most obvious concern is freshness, so it's advisable to work small and complete a study in one sitting when you can.

WORKING FROM PHOTOGRAPHS

Although he and the other Impressionists took an interest in the recently invented medium of photography, Renoir doesn't appear to have worked from photographs, preferring the experience of working from life. As will be expanded on in the coming chapters, Renoir's approach to oil painting owes a lot to the whole experience of his subject being there, in three dimensions, in front of him, so it is essential to gain this experience of working directly from your subject. This is easiest with still life objects and should definitely be tried *en plein air*. This being said, photographs can still be useful, particularly when you have limited time with your subject. For the images of the girl reading (see pages 60–63) I took photographs of my daughter sitting in different rooms of the house; and photographs are definitely useful for constructing multifigure groups.

Photography can have the advantage in certain situations, for instance when you can capture authentic scenes that aren't posed but rather are genuine events. As with all still-life and figure painting, the key to working from photographs is to light your models well, so that your photographic reference will be clear and easy to read; you will be able to make sense of form and space. Another effective way of using photographic reference material is to work from blurred or out-of-focus images, with another, clear version to hand for the final stages of the painting. If you don't have a model, this approach can be a helpful way of tuning in to Impressionism.

WORKING FROM DRAWINGS

Renoir generally didn't work from drawings—often the drawings of his that exist were made after a successful painting and were turned into prints or etchings. A few drawings in preparation for some of his more linear paintings exist; these are clear line drawings, like the two above. If you are new to oil painting, and if you are not especially confident with sketching a composition directly in oil paint, making a quick drawing can be an excellent way of training your eye to frame a scene without any of the mess, the effort or the pressure involved with painting. Use a cut-out viewfinder (see page 19) and sketch both a portrait and a landscape version to see what works best.

SETTING UP YOUR STUDIO
Plein Air *Studio*

When making preparations to work outdoors, much of your planning will revolve around the practical concern of being able to transport materials easily. You will want a small amount of equipment that is light and portable. The weather will impact on you straightaway and it can be highly changeable, necessitating a speed and flexibility to adapt and exploit the changing scene. This can be to your advantage if you can learn to work quickly and summarize your scene with a minimum of marks.

FINDING YOUR STUDIO

Ideally, you will already know exactly where to situate your *plein air* studio because there will be particular viewpoints with which you are familiar and have been looking forward to capturing in paint. If you are working in an unfamiliar environment, don't set up your materials and equipment until you are sure that you're in the best location. It can be useful to draw a few black-and-white thumbnail sketches, just to help you look a little more carefully at what is likely to be included in a particular viewpoint (see pages 36–37: Selecting a Composition for things to consider).

Selecting the most interesting and inspiring composition should be the deciding factor for where to work; however, there will of course be some practical considerations to bear in mind as well. You will probably find it easier to work a little off the beaten track so that you are not in anyone's way and won't be distracted too frequently by interested parties. You will need to be able to stand back from your work and set up an easel, possibly also a folding table, so flat ground is a plus. If the day is one of bright sunshine it can be hard to see exactly what you have just painted with a wet surface reflecting the light, so a spot in a bit of shade looking out to a well-lit scene is ideal.

EASEL

Folding easels are very useful; definitely preferable to holding you painting on your lap—your hands will be free and it makes it possible to stand back and consider your work. Both wooden and metal varieties take a bit of practice to put up. The metal folding easel is usually a sturdier product and has the advantage of legs that can be easily pushed into the ground for extra stability. These easels only really seem to have a structure once your canvas or board is in place. In windier climes such as my native Scotland, however, once the canvas or board is in place it can act like a sail and your easel might take off! One solution is to hang a plastic bag with a few stones in it from the center of the easel (above); this should help to stabilize it.

PALETTES

A small piece of Formica board will be heavy enough to stay put if you are painting in a strong breeze—I find a combination of a heavier palette like this for your paint supplies, that you can leave on the ground, and a small hand-held palette for the mixtures works quite well (below left). Again, if the weather conditions are trying, not having to keep stopping to mix more paint is helpful.

OIL PAINTS & MEDIUMS

The transportable tube of oil paint is synonymous with the Impressionists' ability to go out into the landscape to record their new vision of the world around them. However, it is advisable to limit the number of colors that you take.

A double dipper can be attached to your hand-held palette for linseed oil and turps, and a larger tin or jar will be needed for turps to clean brushes as you work—keep only small quantities that can be exchanged regularly for clean from a securely lidded source. Find a stone to drop into the tin and you will be less likely to knock it over or have the wind do this for you.

CANVAS/BOARD

When working outdoors, it's generally best to work on a fairly small scale—partly because of the wind factor, but also so that you are able to handle an oil composition under the pressure of time. The Impressionist *plein air* canvases tended to be around 16 x 24 inches (40 x 60cm), and the bigger canvases not much larger than 35 inches (90cm) wide.

Transporting the finished but still-wet canvas also presents a challenge. Some older wooden paint boxes have a clever sliding feature in the lid that allows one or two panels to be stored without their wet surfaces touching anything. A cheap and easy alternative is to fashion a simple box for transporting panels of a standard size, using a cardboard box with adapted sides (above).

VIEWFINDER

Cut a simple viewfinder from some card or mounting board with which you can survey your subject matter. It can be used to select the most interesting view, as it will eliminate anything beyond the basic rectangular window (below right). Hold it both horizontally and vertically to consider whether to frame a landscape or portrait view, respectively, and to select a good combination of elements. Once you have decided on your choice of composition, put the viewfinder away— you don't really want to attempt to paint while still looking through the small window.

CHAPTER 2: RENOIR CLOSE UP

Although a key member of the Impressionist movement, Renoir was in many ways closer to his eighteenth-century predecessors in spirit than his contemporaries such as Monet and Manet were. As a young man he had admired the Old Masters in the Louvre, particularly the playful works of Fragonard and Boucher, and in Italy he admired the work of Raphael and Rubens. Painting *en plein air* side by side with Claude Monet, their canvases are similar in their Impressionist style, although each had his own particular interests and emphasis. With time, Renoir's work became more studio-based, more figurative in subject matter and, perhaps stimulated by his appreciation of the artists of the past, far more classical in style than his ultramodern Impressionist contemporaries.

It can be difficult to summarize Renoir's technique, although his paintings are generally characterized by luminous colors, feathery brushstrokes and a host of detailed observation. It seems he explored the whole range of possible ways of handling oil paint—sometimes all within one canvas—but not in a particularly systematic way. During his life, his approaches varied from pure Impressionism, through a spontaneous studio style, passing a crisis of quite uncharacteristic planning, rehearsing and (some might say unsuccessful) execution, to a late mature phase where he excelled in color and touch but, hampered by old age and disability, some of his control and draftsmanship were weakened.

Here, we will look at each of his themes and areas of work to tease out some basic approaches and clarify some of the ways that Renoir exploited the versatile medium of oil paint.

RENOIR CLOSE UP
Landscape & Impressionism

Renoir was at the heart of Impressionism from its inception. Together with Monet, he helped forge this new movement of paintings full of color and light. Their expeditions to paint outdoors in front of their subjects were like a breath of fresh air through the art world of the day. By painting *en plein air*, these artists were not only painting what they saw but they were also painting their whole experience. It was fundamentally transformative to the act of painting just "being there." If you try painting outdoors you will be able to understand some of this just in terms of the practicalities—the changes of scene, of light, people, weather; all meaning that the artist has to learn to work quickly, often employing a combination of what they can see together with what they remember seeing a few minutes earlier. There can be an almost intoxicating element to the *plein air* experience, and everything it entails can lead to a much more vital kind of art—Renoir and Monet's work feels more alive and exciting than that of many of their contemporaries, who methodically built up and refined their images in the studio according to a whole range of conventions and artifices.

Developments in pigments, oil paint in tubes and new ideas of color theory all contributed to the new way of seeing and recording the world. Many of the new vanguard of artists also wanted to escape the problems inherent in the practices of the past Masters—the yellowing effect of linseed oil, the cracking of built-up layers—and Impressionism offered new technical approaches as well as a new aesthetic. In spite of his spontaneous nature, however, Renoir was an advocate of sound technique: "Be a good craftsman," he once said; "It won't stop you being a genius."

Woman with a Parasol in a Garden

A close inspection of *Woman with a Parasol in a Garden* (1875–1876), right, reveals an astonishing range of painterly marks. The initial impression may be of confusion, or lack of clarity, but by standing back a little or blurring your eyes you can better appreciate the sense of light and movement captured in the brushmarks. For this reason this painting is a very good example of the Impressionists' *tache*—the bold dabs of vivid color that do not blend on the canvas but rather sit side by side to build an impression of depth, light and contrast.

The painting's structure is not immediately obvious, but gradually reveals itself as you enter into the picture: a diagonal line of flower heads leads the eye from the bottom left-hand corner into the middle of the painting where the figures are entering the scene, then a series of horizontal blocks of darker bushes and trees recede upward to the top of the painting. The variation in the size of *tache* lends the painting its sense of depth or distance, with the smaller, less distinct marks of the background contrasting with the bold and intricate marks of the bank of flowers in the foreground. The bright, luminous colors, together with touches of reflected light and dark shadows, and the directional marks, are effective in suggesting the particular quality of the day in this garden scene. All of this is very understated and, since the framework is not especially obvious, our attention can be given to the sheer decorative nature of the garden blooms.

The Watering Place

The Watering Place (1873), left, is a good example of Renoir's take on Impressionism. A footpath divides the composition as it climbs from right to left and recedes into the distance, adding a sense of depth to the picture. As with *Woman with a Parasol in a Garden* on page 23, the foreground marks are generally larger and more distinct, while distance is created by softer contrasts of color and tone receding into the background. Vertical marks indicate the stems and leaves of the vegetation, while shorter, horizontal strokes suggest the ground and the footpath. Everything in the image seems to be in motion: the sky, trees and tall grasses are painted with varyingly angled short brush strokes. The feeling of movement is helped further by the contrasts between the layers and qualities of paint used by Renoir.

It is possible to make out from the reproduction the impasto marks that stand out on the surface of the grasses and the leaves of the tree. All this is, of course, much easier and more satisfying to observe in a real painting—so if you can, it is certainly worth seeing some of Renoir's works in the flesh: get close to see the painting surface in a raking light to discern the thicker and thinner painted marks. The thicker brush marks would have been added at a later stage in the painting and floated over darker colors so that they stood out for their contrast in value, as well as being physically raised above the rest of the painted surface due to the more substantial consistency of the paint.

The *alla prima* oil-painting method that is so effective in a painting such as this is best done in a particular sequence or a certain order, which will be explored and deconstructed in the coming chapters. Renoir is also capturing a fleeting moment here: the general form of the tree is first painted thinly and then worked up to a final design that includes the placing of the lightest top-most leaves. The sky invades the tree, the tree breaks out into the sky; their spaces are not clearly distinguished or separate.

In some respects the scene is perhaps not an obvious subject for a landscape. It is a little uneventful and arbitrary even, and there seems to be no apparent structure. This is Renoir breaking with the traditional designs and conventions of artists such as Nicolas Poussin and Claude Lorrain that he learnt from Gleyre.

In some ways Renoir was not naturally a landscape painter at all—he was drawn to painting figures ("Nature leads the artist into loneliness, I want to remain among people," he said). But he painted people with the similar urgency and intensity of "being there"—all the lessons landscape painting had taught him about seizing the essence of his subject and risking all with the painted gestures, he applied to his paintings of figures and groups.

EN PLEIN AIR

- One of the key concerns of Impressionism was the quality of light. Before beginning to paint, take time to really notice the colors of the scene you're observing, and the play of light and shadows on the vegetation.
- With their interest in "being there," the Impressionists virtually invented a new way of seeing; at least in the art world. Elements in the foreground are painted using larger, stronger marks, while the background, painted with smaller, less distinct marks, naturally blurs and recedes. Thus the *tache* mark allows you to create a sense of depth and perspective even without the use of any of the usual structural devices that give a painting scale.

Girls at the Piano

Girls at the Piano (1892), left, was an official commission for the French State, to be hung in the Musée du Luxembourg—a notable honor for any French artist, even though Renoir had to wait until he was nearly 50 before he received it. Renoir's approach to this painting was less spontaneous than many of his earlier compositions, reflecting the formal nature of the commission. He embarked on a series of drawings and studies, and even created at least three other finished versions of the same image, rehearsing and rehearsing it in slightly different ways. One study, for example, has the simplest of backgrounds made up of colors and shapes that, when compared with the illustrated version, obviously relate to a curtain and opening through to another room.

Within this painting there is great variety in the handling of the paint, particularly in the difference between much of the interior and surroundings of the figures—which are treated with thinner paint so that the weave of the canvas is visible in many places—and the thicker, more descriptive handling of clothing, brass candlesticks, ribbons and hair. In these areas the light that shines on a white dress or golden hair has been emphasized by the use of thicker paint that stands out from the canvas surface and, in some cases, has been brightened by a yellow glaze.

In terms of his technique, examining this painting gives us plenty of opportunity to explore Renoir's approaches. But the background to its creation is also telling. Renoir was, according to a critic, "paralyzed" by the idea of the commission and "began the painting five or six times, each time almost identically." For all artists a commission is a double-edged sword—the income is highly attractive, but the imperative to complete a piece of work in a particular way can be utterly inhibiting. In the case of Renoir, who we shall repeatedly see was clearly an intuitive and instinctive painter, the constraints of a commission would be even worse.

PORTRAITS

- Renoir's approach to portraiture was typically almost as spontaneous as that of his landscapes; however the nature of portraiture means that the artist is somewhat restrained. Many of Renoir's portraits (and of the Impressionists in general) were criticized as "unflattering" because of their style. Renoir felt freer in his still lifes, and used techniques developed there in his more careful figure work.

- *Girls at the Piano* is a good example of the importance of context. While many of Renoir's head-and-shoulders paintings depict the subject against a blurred and undefined background, some of his most important works such as this and *Madame Charpentier* (1878), another commissioned portrait, feature elements of the subject's world, telling the viewer more about them. Choice of clothing is important in this respect as well.

Luncheon of the Boating Party

The Impressionists were keen to depict the modern world around them and the city with its busy life. Many were influenced by what they saw in the recently-invented photography. The invention of this new medium forced artists to reconsider the goal of their work—clearly there could be no competition between painting and photography when it came to an accurate depiction of reality. The new aesthetic in the techniques and styling of the Impressionists emphasizes an aspect of the moment, of "being there," that photography cannot capture. But the new medium also inspired contemporary artists to portray a "slice of life"— lively social situations free from formality and order, like the moments captured in photographic snapshots. Renoir clearly had some *joie de vie* and this is nicely illustrated by one of his greatest multifigure compositions, *Luncheon of the Boating Party* (1881), right. "I am doing a picture of a boating party that I have been itching to do for a long time," he wrote to a friend, "...It's a good thing from time to time to attempt something beyond one's powers."

This is a highly animated scene in which many of Renoir's friends can be identified. A gathering of friendship and bonhomie filled with people who posed together in this riverside setting. The painting is epic in its content, including 14 people, a dog, a riverscape (including boats passing) and still-life elements on the table. There is plenty to be said about the content of the painting, but one of the most interesting things about *Luncheon of the Boating Party* is its composition; the strong use of lines, vertical and diagonal, to divide the painting, to draw attention to the parts that Renoir wants you to notice, and effectively to guide your eye around the painting. The eyelines between the people around the table also add plenty of dramatic interest to the painting, and especially help in distinguishing those characters who remain separate from the jovial conversations taking place.

SLICES OF LIFE

- Multifigure compositions such as *Luncheon of the Boating Party* and *Dance at Le Moulin de la Galette* (1876) speak to the Impressionists' desire to depict a "slice of life," or §life as it really was instead of the artfully and rather rigidly composed works that had come before.

- It is likely that Renoir composed multifigure works like this one in composite. While he was not believed to have made studies for the painting beforehand, the canvas was developed slowly, adding models as they were available, and details as it progressed. Yet the end result retains the freshness that characterizes Renoir's work, a feeling of spontaneity and the all-important sense of "being there."

- Renoir's figure group paintings are full of the elements that were important to the Impressionist vision: in *Dance at Le Moulin de la Galette*, for example, the crowd dances under beautiful dappled light. In *Oarsmen at Chatou* (1879), an orange skiff stands out boldly against the complementary blue of the water.

Peaches on a Plate

Peaches on a Plate (1902/1905), above, depicts peaches in a swirl of brush marks, circling around the round table and spiraling inward to the fruits themselves, which in turn are modeled with directional brush marks that follow their spherical forms. This is deftly combined with a perfect observation of the constituent colors that characterize the peach and the way these reds, oranges and yellows dovetail one into the next. Renoir not only precisely records the color of the peaches, contrasting it with the blues and violets in the white tablecloth, but he also manages to capture the soft, delicate texture of their skins, which he achieves through the soft edges he has given each form. If you examine the outlines of each fruit, you will see that either the background colors have been painted into the peach, or the edge has been created by an initial thin layer of paint and so doesn't have the sharpness of more substantially applied oils. This earlier stage of luminous, thinned paint is evident in the gaps that Renoir has left between the brushstrokes in the white cloth. The cream or pink ground in the weave of the canvas

showing through contrasts with the thicker and more opaque whites and blues on top. Significantly there are no gaps in the painting of the fruit; these are solid and modeled fully in three-dimensional colors.

STILL-LIFE TECHNIQUE

- Renoir focused his still-life compositions on arrangements of fruit and flowers. His approach to these subjects was quite free; he experimented to develop techniques that captured their qualities, particularly color and texture.
- The marks Renoir uses describe the subject he is painting, following the direction of their form to give a sense of three-dimensionality.
- As with his landscapes, Renoir uses thicker, brighter paint on the areas of the painting he wants to stand out. Toward the background, the colors are more muted and the paint is allowed to blend more—all helping the background to recede in the eye.

Bouquet of Chrysanthemums

Bouquet of Chrysanthemums (c. 1884), above, is a riot of color and texture—wild, or at least untamed, flowers bursting out of their vase. Renoir has developed a particular kind of radiating brush mark that describes the flowers and the arrangement of their petals, and this pattern or motif is repeated or echoed in the way in which the round vase and even the texture of the background is handled. The unruly petals fighting to sit one on top of the other must have been painted via a similar kind of battle: the thick oil paint of one petal stroke overlays another, mixing a bit and perhaps losing its clarity, so needing to be restated in order to be the most emphatic. By contrast, the background paint is much less substantial and the brush marks are translucent, the paint only just covering the white primer of the canvas.

RENOIR CLOSE UP
Nudes

In his later years Renoir's favorite subject was the nude. "My concern," he said, "has always been to paint nudes as if they were some kind of splendid fruit." He talked of seeking the perfect model, one whose skin could take the light well. Willem De Kooning famously said that flesh was the reason that oil paint was invented, and in this medium Renoir sought to represent and recreate a believable impression of it. The small background figures in some of Renoir's bather compositions, or his rapid impasto studies of nudes, seem to prefigure later artists such as Lucian Freud and Frank Auerbach. Renoir employed different techniques to render skin convincingly, starting with the luminous underpainting; the build up of lighter, thicker paint in parts of the figure, or soft edges where the initial diluted paint layer can still be seen beneath the opaque marks, giving depth and subtlety to the form. Contours of limbs and torsos were carefully described with feathery brush marks working their way round anatomical forms. Renoir's nudes always seem to be a celebration of life and of being alive.

Reclining Odalisque

Although not a nude, *Reclining Odalisque* (1917–1919), below, gives some useful insights into Renoir's painting process. The model is probably Gabrielle (his wife's cousin), so her hair would likely eventually have been dark, had the painting been taken further. We can see that Renoir has laid down some rich red in the hair, which would show through the next scumbled, translucent layer of dark paint to give the necessary warmth for the hair to harmonize with the other skin colors. The treatment of the flesh may also be unfinished, or preparatory. Here we see an overall, harmonizing cream coloring thinly filling the areas of exposed arms, legs and head. These are outlined (and warmed) with a red-brown line. In the center of these areas, a thicker trail of a warm white tint has been dragged along the contours of the limbs and head. This line stands out, giving form to the rounded parts of the figure, and they would stand out even more if another layer of similar warm pale skin color was applied across and alongside them. Meanwhile, the background has been painted more thinly, and the distinction between the treatment of the surroundings and that of the figure would be maintained in subsequent stages of the painting—were there to be any.

PAINTING FLESH

- Renoir's early nudes, such as *Nude in Sunlight* (1876) are replete with Impressionist concerns. Painted out of doors, these paintings are more naturalistic and full of light.
- His later nudes, such as *Bather and Maid* (right) and *The Bathers (Les Baigneuses*, 1918–1919) are far more classical in execution, showing the influence of Titian and Rubens on Renoir's later work. These works depict mythological, timeless scenes, often in Mediterranean settings. The women in these paintings are free and sensual, represented as being at one with nature in an earthly paradise, reflecting Renoir's unfailingly positive outlook on life.
- By developing his paintings through a series of layers, Renoir's compositions come together in a harmonious way. The first thin, translucent layers are not obliterated by the later opaque stages, but used to bring colors together, to give luminosity, or to allow the background to recede.

Bather and Maid (La Toilette)

Bather and Maid (La Toilette) (c. 1900), above, shows a more highly worked and finished nude. A second figure arranges the nude's hair and a familiar riverside and landscape setting has been developed allowing Renoir to contrast the warm skin colors with nature's cool blues and greens. The painting is filled with a dreamy atmosphere of halcyon days.

In contrast with his earlier nudes, *Bather and Maid* would have been painted in the studio, and its classical composition marks a break from Impressionism. These later nudes, mythological figures in idealized settings, are an expression of Renoir's wish to paint beautiful and uplifting images. In spite of being crippled and in pain, there is no hint of bitterness or despair in his luminous, life-affirming work.

CHAPTER 3: *PLEIN AIR* RENOIR

The Impressionist vision was deeply connected with the experience of the outdoors, as opposed to the artificial and controlled methods of the studio. Artists before had painted outdoors, but often just to collect studies for use in larger, contrived compositions back in the studio. Many were well aware of the artifice this involved—it was art, after all—but accepted that the vitality and expression of these *plein air* studies would have to be tidied up and civilized in pictures bound for exhibition. Monet and Renoir painted together at the river, capturing the fleeting effects of the light and weather, and the people enjoying themselves on Sunday afternoons. The temporary nature of their subjects—always moving and changing—inspired a spontaneous approach to the way they handled the oil paint.

In this chapter we will look particularly at *alla prima* oil painting—the all-at-once, wet-on-wet handling of the medium. The most challenging aspect of oil paint may well be the best thing about it as well: when you apply oils to a canvas already covered with wet paint, colors mix and will eventually muddy. Learning to control the extent of this mixing, and enjoying the softening effects as one area subtly blends with the next, can produce the most exciting and surprising results.

Alla prima painting allows an overall command of the whole picture because the painting is intended to be begun and finished all in one session. It calls for a virtuoso handling of the material; a boldness in approach that can bring out an inspired response. It's all about edges—the soft, blended edges, and those that are more sharply defined. Being able to control these edges and the inevitable mixing of the paint requires some forethought in your preparation and a decisive handling of the material. There is something fundamental to the whole artistic endeavor in the *alla prima* approach: you begin in a generalized way and gradually work toward a particular emphasis as the work reaches its resolution. Beyond this, it also involves a degree of faith; a readiness to work with accidents and discoveries. Good preparation and a certain amount of organization in the execution make it possible to carry this risky activity much further than you might imagine. This chapter outlines the steps worth taking in order to accomplish confident and inspired *alla prima* oil painting—and *plein air* work in general.

PLEIN AIR RENOIR
Selecting a Composition

Selecting a composition to paint can be done by looking through a simple viewfinder held horizontally or vertically in front of you (below). It's worth trying out both to determine whether your subject is best suited to a landscape or portrait format. Look in all directions to see what presents itself inside your rectangular window. Compare the view *contre jour* (against the light) with having the light behind you, shining onto the scene; depending on direction of the light, you will find you get quite different experiences. Alternatively, more preparation and deliberation can be made by first making small thumbnail sketches. Renoir would not have prepared with studies, but sketches can be a helpful reference. These might be line drawings to establish the basic design of shapes and patterns, or tonal studies that will help with the patterns of light and shade—or both.

Renoir's compositions often included a pathway into the distance, which can be a useful device for adding depth to a composition. Another feature he commonly employed was framing the view with the trunk and overhanging branches of a tree. Here, the bounds of the tree act as a scale to which other points of the picture can be compared. When you choose your composition, try to think in terms of what will give your painting depth: perhaps a horizon with a hill or trees on it, a pathway or line of trees, or forms in the foreground, such as a tree, a fence or a gate, to give a sense of perspective to smaller, more distant elements. Also consider the range of colors that will be included within your picture frame. Some people tire of "all that green" in their landscape efforts, so consider looking for variety in your chosen composition, or at least variety in the greens you will have to tackle.

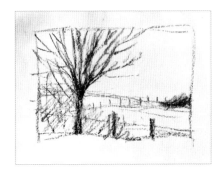

The thumbnail sketches above show examples of possible compositions for a scene I found while wandering down the path at Skipness, Argyll, Scotland. The sketches have been made on a very small scale using thin sticks of willow charcoal. Working in this way and with this medium will help you effectively summarize what you are seeing; willow is a quick, fluid medium, and it seems to offer a very atmospheric interpretation of the subject. The soft, hazy quality of the charcoal is itself a little reminiscent of the Impressionist style in oil paint, making it an ideal medium to sketch with.

Top left: A tree on the left frames the composition. The horizon is fairly low, broken by a pattern of fields and trees on the right-hand side up to the edge of horizon. A fence crosses the frame diagonally, receding in to the distance.

Top center: A view through to the sea and the Isle of Arran sitting high on the horizon. A tree takes up the right-hand side of the frame, and woods in the middle ground to the left give perspective. In foreground are sheep, and a ruined chapel in the middle-distance.

Top right: Slightly different from the previous, this time from farther back, the trees that took up the whole right-hand side of the frame are now positioned in the middle distance. They still help with depth, the woods on the left appearing smaller with perspective. It is worth moving around and viewing the same scene from different angles to see what works best—which view is the most interesting or appealing?

Bottom left: A view up a path through trees, with a sloping, tree-lined horizon behind, lines of perspective in the field on the right, fence posts and a textured forground.

Bottom center and bottom right: Sometimes the attempt to fit the view into the small sketch can be helped by drawing the scene first and then adding the frame afterward.

The exercise of trying to fit a whole landscape scene into a small rectangle usually proves quite frustrating at first. You may struggle to condense the subject, and it will often end up too big and too involved for your thumbnail scale—but it is an extremely valuable process to go through. Attempting to simplify the scene before you into a minimum of marks and a very small format will help you to see the entire subject and not just parts of it. In this way you will have a much greater grip on the entirety of your landscape and will therefore be able to paint a much more coherent picture, rather than being overwhelmed by the details as can so often happen. Renoir did not seem to make many such investigations of his landscape subject, instead launching directly into the painting, but it should be noted that he was practiced in the art of "seeing" his subjects without first having to rehearse them in a drawing. Some of the work of fitting the scene onto canvas can also be done at the initial diluted-paint stage; however, the ability to picture a composition takes practice and experience. Making these simple thumbnails and the learning art of condensing your subject will train you to be able to begin a composition in paint.

PLEIN AIR RENOIR
Starting the Composition

Renoir generally began his paintings with a subtle, tentative exploration of the colors presented by the scene. Thinned oil paints were distributed loosely across the canvas as he explored how the colors worked together. Renoir called the diluted paint his "juice." This is an instinctive process, which you should try. If you are uncertain where to start, a tonal thumbnail sketch works well as a springboard for beginning with the darker colors that you have observed. Alternatively, you might select a dominant color—during a certain phase, Renoir began his paintings with cobalt blue for the shadows and arranged the entire composition around that hue. This view of an island across the sea shows how you can easily begin your composition from a very simple juice base.

A brown juice is first spread out to denote some of the main areas (above). This diluted paint should be thin and transparent. It can help to start with a dark, warm juice to identify the main darker tonal regions, as I have done here.

Viridian and brown, chrome yellow and viridian, cobalt blue and red—all these mixtures of oil paint produce bright, transparent colors that encourage a vibrancy in the opaque mixtures that will be applied on top, so don't be afraid if it looks garish at this stage (below). A balance is struck between the warm brown colors of the trees and island and the cool greens and blues in the grass, water and sky.

This is now ready for the next stage of the painting, when you will begin to apply some opaque colors.

SURFACE OF THE CANVAS

Wherever you begin, with this organic way of developing a painting it is, in part, just a question of time before the various colors and tones begin to gel and to give you back a faint vision of what the painting might become.

Renoir usually began on a white, fine-grained canvas surface. By beginning on white, the transparent colors appear quite luminous, and the overall color scheme may be bright in response to this unifying base. The top row of images, above, are examples of a painting developed from a white ground.

At times, Renoir also used other pale off-white grounds to begin his paintings on, occasionally adopting a red-brown base in the style of the landscape painters of previous generations, notably Constable. Being essentially complementary, the cool blues and greens of the sky and vegetation sing out on this layer—both standing out as opposite, and being warmed by the unifying effect of the underlayers.

A second example of a painting begun on a beige or pale brown surface is illustrated in the second row of images, above. An overall feeling of warmth pervades this image. Cool colors like blues and greens stand out on the warm underlayer and in consequence the feeling of daylight is strengthened. Warmer colors will, however, need to be very colorful if you want them to stand out against a semi-transparent brown ground.

PLEIN AIR RENOIR
Developing the Painting

PREPARING THE PALETTE

For the initial stage of the painting using thinned paint, a minimal amount of mixing is required, and only small quantities will be needed. It is fine to use your brush to pick and mix pure colors together, both on the palette and directly on the surface of the canvas. However, the next stage of the painting will involve applying larger quantities of thicker paint, premixed into specific main colors: you will need a variety of light and dark, bright and muted colors. These are much harder to mix with the brush, as you will need good amounts that can be picked up on the tip of a clean, dry brush and deposited on the surface of the picture, so it's a good idea to use a palette knife to mix your stock colors. If your brush has already been used for mixing paint it won't be clean enough to pick up fresh colors. As will soon become clear, the key to managing *alla prima* painting, and creating the best conditions for painting in a spontaneous way, is having a clear set of ready mixed colors to reach for. It is important to know exactly what is going on the end of your brush and to be decisive in your approach—both of which can become harder as pigments begin to mix accidently on the surface of the painting. Make it easier for yourself to begin by starting with a clear, clean palette with a good range of colors already mixed.

The image below left shows a palette prepared with a good range of colors with which to begin a landscape. This palette may appear limited, but it will produce families of colors that have been mixed from each other and are therefore related, helping to achieve a harmony in the finished piece. The sky, for example, may be mixed from cobalt and white, with green for a lighter hue and red for a darker one; your greens and other colors will also be adapted in a similar way.

Below right, you see a separate palette prepared with the thinned paint, or juice. This will contain fewer colors, as variations in tone and even brightness can be achieved simply by spreading paint out or mixing on the canvas.

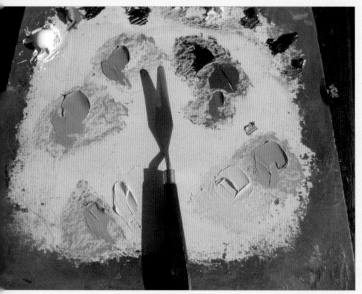

40

WORKING IN A CERTAIN ORDER

Once your canvas has been covered with the juice to suggest the color scheme and the basic tonal pattern of the composition, it can be helpful to think about the order in which you are going to apply the thicker and more opaque paint. Establishing some of the darker colors first, for example, means that their strength can be maintained through the process, as other colors will be painted around them—thus avoiding unnecessary mixing. The colors will naturally mix and muddy along the way, but if some unblended darks remain, they can be topped up at a later stage.

It can also be a good policy to work from the background, or the distant subject matter, toward the foreground. This will often mean using an increasing amount of paint and, as Renoir might have done, larger brushstrokes as you come to the foreground to denote subjects that are nearer.

Sometimes the order in which you paint things relates to the way in which they are situated in the landscape: for instance it is sensible to paint the distant hill before you paint the tree that stands in the foreground in front of it (unless this is intended to be a large, dark form—in silhouette, perhaps—as mentioned); or the riverbed before the reflective surface of the water above it, and so on.

These are only general suggestions to help you begin; the process will vary from canvas to canvas, and ideally, especially as you become more familiar with the medium, it will be more varied and spontaneous, and less linear than this.

PAINTING THE SKY

The detail of a cloudy sky (above) is a good example of how you might think about building up a certain area of the painting according to both the nature of the subject and the demands of *alla prima* painting.

First, cobalt blue is spread out loosely and with varying intensity—thinner paint gives a fainter color. Then opaque colors (based on cobalt blue and Naples yellow) are added to strengthen the sky color, and are also now used for the lighter clouds. By painting the clouds more thickly and after, or on top of, the sky, they stand out as more substantial—just as they do in life. The pale mixtures can be floated with almost no mixing for a bright effect, or blended a little on the painting surface in order to subdue their effect and create the subtle transitions from light to dark cloud colors.

PLEIN AIR RENOIR
Masterclass: Arran from Skipness

Once you have established your juice beginning and you're preparing to start working up the canvas with thicker paint, you can save yourself a great deal of trouble by considering the best order in which to go about this. As mentioned on the previous page, there is no one right order or set of rules to follow. Each canvas is different, and you will find that the process will largely be a matter of responding to unexpected demands and results that arise as you work. Having at least some kind of plan to go by before you start slapping on paint will stand you in good stead, though: it can potentially save you a lot of work, and hopefully will also prevent you from getting too caught up in the details. This Masterclass, continuing from the juice beginning on page 38, offers a practical demonstration of some of the considerations involved in working up a painting in a particular order.

1

The first layer of opaque paint is applied to the areas of sky and grass. Yellows have been added to the paint mixtures to bring out a vibrancy at least as strong as the luminous transparent layer.

2

Warm darks are strengthened in the fenceposts and the trees. These are foreground elements, so making them stronger will help with the depth of the composition: they stand out and the background fields and sky recede.

3

Next, the sky is blocked in with a few variations on cobalt blue, with white and a touch of viridian—all these variations have been pre-mixed on a Formica palette. The water is built up with short horizontal marks. Some further details are added to the foreground, and clouds are added to the sky.

4

The island is made opaque using fairly rough marks—gaps left between marks are fine. Clouds are added to the sky, and the fenceposts modeled.

5

More foreground details are added, with a variety of lighter and darker hues added to the bluebell leaves at the bottom of the frame. The water is slightly modified, and the tree is developed further with more warm and lighter branches and leaves.

6

Smaller modifications and developments of color are made all around the composition, including some warm greens to depict the leaves on the tree, further modeling to the fenceposts, and more work on the distant island and the sky.

At this stage in the development of a painting, often the best approach involves moving around the composition and working on several different areas. It can be helpful to establish a part of the foreground at the same time as working on something in the distance, so that there is a way of judging how each new development fits into the overall composition. Try not to overwork any part in particular, but move around developing everything simultaneously.

PLEIN AIR RENOIR
Brush Technique & Detail

BUILDING THE COMPOSITION

One of the features that make Renoir's paintings so popular is the fine detail and careful observation of the way things appear. This seems to demonstrate a love of handling oil paint and a delight in the challenge of rendering all things in this magical medium.

It should be stressed, however, that Renoir knew when was the right time to begin to concentrate on the details in his paintings. He knew that first the composition had to be set out to his satisfaction, and that the color scheme also needed to be fairly clear. In other words, the stage needed to be set before the specific fine observations and local colors and variations could be developed. The inexperienced painter is inclined to focus immediately on detail and produce an image in which these observations have no context, or else jump around from one detail to another to produce an image that ultimately isn't coherent to the viewer.

As we have seen, the thinned wash layer that the painting began with was an excellent way for Renoir to identify his colors and allow them to mix and harmonize; it also provided a unifying luminous underpainting that held together the more thickly painted opaque observations that would be added on top of it. In the examples at right you can see once more how a composition can be built from and around this base, ready for the next stage when you will begin to refine the painting, adding emphasis and detail, working toward a finished piece.

Here, I begin with a monochrome blue wash to define the shape of the building and its immediate grass surroundings (top). Then, using the Impressionist *tache*, the chapel, its wall and the gravestones are all begun, using a dark blue-green for shade on the grass, and a lighter, more yellow green to mark highlights (middle). The use of short, discrete brush marks with gaps allowing the blue underpainting to show through has a unifying effect, and it also helps to suggest the direction in which subsequent additions of color might be taken. The shadows on the grass could be varieties of blue-green, for instance, and the shaded areas of stonework might take on a blue-gray tone. At the next stage (bottom) these colors are applied with a short brush mark, and other areas are also treated with appropriate heightened colors.

The blue that begins the painting, restated in the shadows, also helps to emphasize the complementary opposites of the colors used in the brickwork. These warmer oranges and browns can be exaggerated as a response to this heightened blue, and they will stand out all the more strongly.

ADDING DETAILS

Once you have established the transparent layer to your satisfaction, it is time to begin working up the details with thicker, opaque paint. The Impressionist *tache* was a distinct short stroke, often following the contours of the form— horizontal marks used for floors and water, vertical for walls, vegetation and so on. Depending on whether a clear, sharp mark or touch of definition is required, or if a softer, blended effect is sought, the degree of mixing between strokes can be controlled by how much paint is worked in.

Holding the brush parallel to the painting surface means that fresh color can be floated on top of the wet paint, with minimal mixing. Old brushes are not very good at this: if they are short-haired and worn out, they will lift off what is there and deposit nothing. Renoir was fastidious in destroying worn brushes just in case he should start to use one by mistake.

Now we will look at some studies of various landscape elements in their stages, from the dilute, transparent stage through the establishment of forms, often with darker colors, to laying in, or floating on the surface, lighter and brighter colors. Sometimes there is a logic to the order in which paint is applied; for example, the top layer of lichen on a tree's bark will be applied last.

TREE

This study begins with a loose impression of the main colors in the tree and its surroundings, resisting the temptation to define and outline the major forms (left).

Starting with dark and mid-tone colors, paint is dragged along the lengths of the branches and trunk (center). Details of the ground are added, with marks varying in size from large to small, giving the suggestion of depth—the smaller marks indicate the background receding.

The thicker top layer of paint is applied in such a way as to emulate the texture of the lichen on tree's surface; floated onto wet paint, it sits delicately on top, almost in the way that lichen clings to a tree (right). I used square hog hair brushes in sizes 4 and 6, held almost parallel with the surface of the painting and turned in the hand to vary the mark and to capture something of the varied pattern of bark. The grass is built up with brighter greens, stippled or dabbed onto the painting and then topped up with some short, vertical marks.

SHEEP

In the first step, the basic form of the animal is hinted at with diluted paint (top).

Color is built up in stages from the darkest, through the middle color, to the (almost) lightest. The edges of the sheep are softened by the remaining brown of the first stage. When more opaque paint is used on the surrounding grass, the creature can be defined further—although this should be considered carefully. In the context of a larger composition, it might be appropriate to leave these soft edges so that the sheep merges a little with the background and doesn't stand out as the most important part of the painting (middle).

More lighter tones and details are added to help define the form of the sheep, and the opaque background colors help refine the animal to make it a little more sheep-like. They also make it stand out more prominently (bottom).

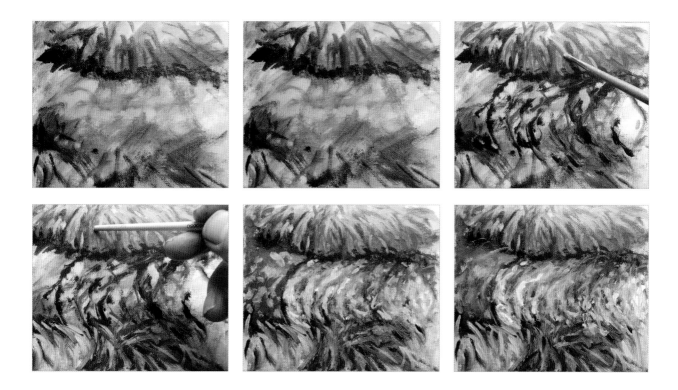

RIVER

It can be useful to think of this subject in terms of layers—the riverbed, the water and then the surface of the water—and to build the paint up according to this sequence. Burnt umber was spread thinly for the dilute underpainting of the muddy bed, with some greens put in for the banks (top left).

Thicker darks are now applied along the edge of the banks to represent the shadows under the vegetation and between leaves of grass (top center).

Dark shadows are applied to the water's surface and the banks are made more substantial with opaque greens and yellow-greens. The side of no. 4 square brush is used for painting short, curved strokes reflecting the shape of the grass (top right).

Scraping into the wet leaves with a brush handle helps to loosen them up and make brushstrokes less obvious, giving a more natural effect (bottom left).

The light reflected on the surface of the water is made with a mixture of white and cobalt blue, so that its cool quality stands out from the dark warm brown of the riverbed. It is applied thickly and sits on the surface of the painting so that it really stands out (bottom center).

A bit more scratching with the brush handle creates the movement, blurring and disorder of the running water (bottom right). It is important that there are gaps between each of the layers and all of these marks, so that the first layer of the riverbed still appears where the paint is thinner or more spread out.

PLEIN AIR RENOIR
Masterclass: Daffodils & View Through Trees

FINAL EMPHASIS

Many people give up on an oil painting just at the moment that all their efforts could turn into a resolved and exciting painting. At this point the artist is often tired, their palette pretty chaotic, and in desperation they reach for muddied colors—even the wrong colors—which they hope will do the trick. A key part of successful *alla prima* painting, however, is knowing exactly what is on the tip of your brush and knowing how and where you want to use it. So now it may be time to take a break, to stand back and assess your palette, as well as your painting. Take the time to mix some more of the required colors and try to be selective about what aspects of the painting really need attention. You may be seeing more and more detail and complexity as you get to know your subject better—but which details will be significant in bringing your painting to a final resolution?

The essential thing at this stage is to recognize what emphasis is needed to transform a rough painting into a finished piece. It is often an addition of highlights, more fresh, clean colors or dark accents that are needed to draw attention to certain key areas; often the artist has become frustrated with increasingly muddied paint that has made everything become rather soft and undefined. Restating some contrasts of tone and color can work very well at this stage, when they combine with the mid-tones and muted colors that have been generated by the paint being worked together in the *alla prima* process. Sometimes it is useful to have made a preparatory sketch in charcoal or pencil for your painting. Made quickly and with a minimum of marks, these sketches should contain little more than what is essential to the composition; a glance at this can remind you of what you first saw in the subject—and therefore of what should be emphasized at this last stage.

The outdoors presents all sorts of challenges: changing light and weather, the wind, insects and distracting passersby . . . And yet these apparent obstacles can all help encourage a speedy and decisive approach to painting. Impressionism was all about capturing fleeting moments, the flickering light and changable conditions of the open air. Sometimes the work you have already done, building the picture into a general scene, can be viewed simply as the necessary preparation that makes it possible to actually capture a split-second moment in time on your canvas—and this will be the final emphasis you're looking for. Having observed the clouds and laid down some basic colors and shapes in the sky, you now have the opportunity to paint in a particularly nice cloud that has appeared at just that moment, or perhaps the bend of a tree in the wind, for example; this is what you're looking for to give a conclusion to your painting.

1

A spot on a daffodil-lined road with a view through the trees to the hills beyond is chosen to begin the composition. Under the trees there is shade from the full sunlight, and my easel is set up off the road, out of the way of traffic.

2

Using the viewfinder, I decide on a composition framed by two larger trees— one slightly nearer than the other so that they don't look too symmetrical and contrived—across the fields to the hills, with smaller trees in the distance.

3

Now the general design is sketched in with diluted colors, thinned with a mixture of turps and linseed oil. Cobalt is used for the sky, burnt umber and ocher for the trees and a mix of chrome yellow and viridian for the field. Daffodil leaves are suggested with greens made from viridian and umber, or viridian and chrome yellow, with the flowers dabbed in with yellow.

4

A good example of one of the difficulties of working en plein air, the next stage is less easy to see due to the sun reflecting off the surface of the canvas. With this layer of opaque paint, the sky is painted in with blues from cobalt and white, as well as some Naples yellow in the clouds. More ocher and umber is added for the trees—short, vertical marks capture the texture and pattern of the bark. The field is blocked in with a combination of a warm green (viridian, ocher and white) and a cool green (viridian, chrome and white), with short, wide brushstrokes. The daffodil leaves are defined with waving vertical lines, tapering at the top by turning the brush on its side before lifting it off the canvas.

5

I move around the canvas, building up and varying some of the colors, keeping a good balance between foreground and background work and not being drawn into details yet. There is enough contrast and variety in the foreground trees and flowers to make them come forward, and the blue of the sky seen through the frame of the trees recedes. There are now just the middle-ground trees to fit into this overall effect.

6

The middle-ground trees are established by painting their branches into wet sky colors. You don't want to overly define mid-distance features, but let them fade slightly into the background. A thin silver birch tree in the foreground is also developed with a gray color scheme.

7

Daffodils are worked up in the foreground. Finer leaf shapes are painted in with a sable brush that can describe thinner lines than the hog hair. The sable brush also has a calligraphic quality that captures the bending, waving leaves of the flower. Flower heads are also touched in with a sable—the back row is fairly indistinct, but several clearly drawn daffodil flowers can

be made out in the front. Here, the alla prima *approach really takes off: the warm yellow used for the flowers can be painted wet into the greens of the leaves and be cooled down, even muted by them. When a fresh touch of the same yellow is floated on the mixed yellow, it stands out as a brighter part of the flower. Renoir would have noted these sorts of effects and used his experience to employ them where he knew they would be effective—but they can also be discovered just through an instinctive use of the wet oil paints.*

8

Other areas are worked on in a specific way, adding detail and description. More variety is added to the bark of the left-hand tree with its mossy base, and also to the silver birch.

1 COMPOSITION

The only way to develop your skills at finding and sketching a composition is practice. It doesn't matter what media you use—this exercise is all about learning how to find and frame a composition and the elements within it—so for now just make quick sketches in charcoal or pencil.

Making line drawings will help you to pick out the most essential characteristics of the scene and render them quickly. Particularly important are lines that give scale and perspective: the horizon, hills, fences, rivers, trees and so on. Use pencil for this and don't worry too much about including textural details.

Now add tone and some more textural detail using willow charcoal, which is the ideal medium for evoking atmosphere in an Impressionist manner. Look for the darkest and lightest tones first. Be quick in the way you render detail, too—spend no longer than five minutes doing this. Think about particular marks to make; lines that suggest the direction or contour of the land, for example.

2 WORKING IN LAYERS

Take photographs of various features in the landscape such as trees, rocks, flowering plants and so on, and back in the studio make small studies of them painting in the "particular order" we've looked at throughout this chapter (see in particular page 41 and the examples on pages 45–47).

Consider how you can deconstruct the subject into layers and elements that are best tackled in a certain way. For example, paint the trunk of the tree before you apply the rough texture of the bark and add the lichen on top as a final layer. Or, for a stormy sky, you will need to combine watery sky qualities with more solid-looking clouds. Choose things in the landscape that will challenge you to find inventive and varied ways of generating painted marks.

CHAPTER 4 : PORTRAITS

Renoir insisted that he was a figure painter and, in spite of his Impressionist apprenticeship spent capturing the landscape *en plein air* alongside his colleague Monet, his true nature seems to be most clearly expressed in the very personal, joyful and uplifting images of his family and close friends, and of course the female figure. Indeed, it was a particular portrait of Madame Charpentier and her children that made Renoir's name as a painter and generated further commissions.

In this chapter we will examine the ways in which Renoir began and developed his portrait compositions, the sorts of poses he chose for his subjects and the choice of background and setting for the model. There will also be some in-depth examination of the process by which faces, features and hair are developed, and an explanation of the particular forms and characteristics of these features that Renoir was endeavoring to represent.

PORTRAITS
Brush Technique: Two Stages

In terms of technique, the approach Renoir took to his portrait paintings was not dissimilar to his landscapes conducted *en plein air*. A painting began with a roughly sketched juice layer, where basic shapes and colors were laid down, and further successive layers of diluted paint were built up to the point that he was ready to begin laying on opaque details, highlights and emphases. It will be worth going through the whole process in order to see how you might approach a portrait painting in this way, and then, when we come to the stage of thicker, more opaque paint, to investigate what kind of brush marks and techniques might be employed for best effect.

FIRST STAGE: THE "WATERCOLORIST"

The first stage of Renoir's work was generally an experimental investigation of the colors and shapes of his subject. Touches of color applied all over the painting in an apparently random way acted like a map of the scene before him, but it was not a prescriptive plan—the edges of the subject were not defined, and the process was a gradual discovery of these forms. In this process, the colors laid down would mix and overlap, making the edges of each form soft transitions from background to subject, or from one area to another.

The dilute paint used at this stage—a thinned mix of oil paint, linseed oil and turps—can be applied with a soft brush, like watercolors (top). The soft hairs of the brush soak up the liquid paint, which can then be spread around in a fluid way. A stiff hog hair brush can also be used, if you prefer. At times, Renoir also began his painting by rubbing the colors in with a rag and then applying more dilute paint with a brush.

In the subsequent layers, Renoir would attempt to bring the darker colors to their full strength, as well as the mid-tone areas, using thicker paint. It was also at this stage of painting a face that Renoir would begin to indicate the lines of the eyes using a dark, diluted color (brown or black) and possibly some definition to the nose in the same way, as well as the mouth with a dark and rich red. Here, I used a thin sable brush to draw in some lines, beginning to define the main features and giving a shadowed edge to the gardener's woolly hat (bottom).

SECOND STAGE: DESCRIPTIVE MARKS

The background color is strengthened and the first layer of thicker paint is applied to the the hat and to highlights of the face and clothing: the painting is ready for the next stages in opaque paint. The next steps of Renoir's paintings appear to have been done with thicker paint and applied with hog hair brushes. The stiff bristles of the hog hair pick up a dollop of pre-mixed color on the tip of the brush and deposit it in a descriptive way. With these kinds of marks, Renoir was almost drawing with the paint: a short arc described an eyelid, a dot is a pupil, a vertical line for the front of a nose—and so on. These marks should be as simple as possible; skip to pages 68–71 for more detail on painting the features of the face.

Some of the work in these stages would have been done *alla prima*. When painting wet-on-wet, managing the blending of different colors is best done in a fairly systematic way—the darker colors applied first, then mid-tones laid into them and then a final emphasis of the lightest or brightest color. The degree to which these colors blend can be controlled by the brush technique—the extent to which paint is worked in by pressing the brush harder onto the wet canvas, as opposed to lightly floating the new color on the surface of the wet paint so that it barely merges with what is beneath it. Holding the brush parallel to the canvas and using new brushes and fresh, unmuddied paint will help limit the extent of the mixing.

Although it is wise to think about the order you are going to apply your paints before you actually do it, Renoir's use of thicker opaque paints in the next stages of the painting was generally not systematic or predictable; he used a variety of techniques, colors and so on within one canvas. But this does not mean that his approach was abitrary; he would have known the different kinds of effects different techniques would be likely to have on the canvas and employ them according to what he wanted to achieve, and what the painting itself suggested. It is certainly worth practicing techniques like glazing, scumbling and *alla prima*, using both thick impasto paint and thin transparent paint, until you feel familiar with them and know how to use them effectively. We look at these separate techniques in more detail in Chapter 7, pages 110–115.

BRUSH TECHNIQUE IN PORTRAITURE

In your approach to portraiture, remember that although your canvas is flat, your subject is not—the challenge is in making marks that will render the particular qualities of your subject in a convincing (if not necessarily realistic) way.

This detail of the gardener's head shows a range in the ways that the paint has been applied to describe the contours and features of this particular face (top). For example, when painting the forehead, think of it as a broad, horizontal plane that curves slightly at each side, and paint short brushstrokes that describe this arc.

The cheekbone is a kind of shelf that stands out from the cheek and continues back toward the ear. Short brushstrokes that go across the front of the cheek can be curved upward and lead back toward the ear to help sculpt the anatomy of the skull beneath the skin.

The front of the nose is best thought of as a long narrow plane from the bridge to the tip, and long brushstrokes following this direction will help this plane to stand out. The shadow areas of this face contain a variety of colors, and it is a good idea to allow these to blend a little by pressing the wet paint into the wet surface; this will make the shadows appear more subtle and quiet.

When painting the lighter areas, which you probably want to stand out, separate, discrete brush marks of different color and tone when placed side by side will stand out strongly. This can be done with drier oil paint, which sits distinctly on the surface with feathery edges, or by using wetter paint applied with a thin brush with gaps left between the strokes.

You can modify oil paint to achieve a drier, less oily consistency by laying it onto blotting paper and leaving it overnight (bottom). By doing this, some of the oil is drawn out of the paint and the resulting product is drier and a little bit like pastel. It can produce the feathery brush mark more easily than wetter paint.

DETAILS IN OPAQUE

As the painting continues, thicker paint has been pre-mixed on the palette into sets of color, with a range of light, dark and middle tones.

A feathery brushstroke is used to apply the modified, drier oil paint (described on the previous page) to the skin, in an attempt to suggest the contours of the face and the weathered quality of the skin (top left). Notice that when the paint is applied with these discrete brushstrokes, there are gaps between each mark through which the earlier transparent layer can still been seen. This helps give the painting depth and is an excellent way of representing the complexities of skin. The surface of skin is both subtly translucent and reflective, hence the difficulty in rendering it convincingly in paint. Renoir's layers of transparent and opaque paint are a wonderful and loose solution to this problem.

By contrast, in the detail of the gardener's hat (top right) you can see how the thicker opaque paint has a wetter consistency, and as a variety of lighter and darker shades of the blue are applied there is some mixing of the colors on the painting surface. The *alla prima* approach always produces exciting results, and these results can be controlled to some extent by painting in a certain order, as we have already seen. Here, the dark, duller blues are applied first, then the mid-tones and lastly the lightest. The pale blue tints comprise the thickest layer—these are the areas I want to stand out the most—and they are floated on the surface of the other wet paint. By moving the brush in slightly different directions, it is possible to describe, and almost sculpt, the ribbing of the woollen hat.

At the next stage, further layers of both wet and dry thick paint are built up in the face and clothing (bottom right). Notice that no more has been done to the thin background color so that the head stands out more and more from its setting, but the edges of the head and shoulder remain soft and undefined in many places.

PAINT HANDLING & CONSISTENCY

Renoir exploited the enormous potential for variety within the medium of oil paint, and he seems not to have been terribly systematic in his approach to building a painting up, instead painting in a spontaneous and explorative manner. As we have seen, his paintings usually began with the dilute, transparent and fairly experimental layers of myriad different colors, followed by a strengthening of middle and darker tones as he began to define the forms. After this, his use of thicker, more opaque colors, both of wet and dry consistencies, was less predictable.

Some areas of finished canvases appear to have been worked and reworked, with a build-up of oily layers—notably faces that may have caused him difficulty. Other areas were handled using a spontaneous *alla prima* approach, with which he vigorously rendered clothing and furnishings in an instinctive way. Flesh was often rendered in a gradual and methodical manner—fine, feathery strokes applied with a thin brush in a way that softly modeled the contours of a face or the anatomy of a nude.

This Masterclass explores the whole process of working a composition up from juice layer to final emphasis, demonstrating how various mark-making techniques and consistencies of paint may be used for differnt purposes.

1

The model is posed in a window seat, reading her book, with the light coming in from the left. In order to keep the arrangement of the figure and its setting clear, I first paint in the wooden panel behind the girl's head—thus defining the top part of the figure. I am sure that Renoir would have been much less specific in his laying down of the initial transparent colors, though!

2

As I begin to add other areas, gradually building a roughly defined form, the white ground of the primed canvas shows through and illuminates the thin colors used at this stage.

3

The process continues quite quickly and loosely until the whole canvas is covered with this thin layer.

4

When the first layer of dilute oil paint is dry—this should only take about ten minutes with a heater—another transparent layer is painted across different parts of the painting in warm hues. This layer suggests the shadows and darker planes, beginning to model the forms into a more three-dimensional appearance.

5

The next layer, a cool green transparent wash, made using a very small amount of paint diluted with turpentine so that it has a light, transparent consistency, does a similar job to the layer applied in Step 4. In some places it neutralizes the warm red-brown layer, while in others the colors stand out in their own right. This adds weight and depth to the color scheme.

6–7

A thin sable brush is used to delineate the features and to add some definition to the hands. From now on most of the paint applied will be thicker and—crucially—opaque.

8

Now, fairly thick white paint is applied with a stiff hog hair brush to the folds of the dress. This will help emphasize the raised parts of the material—the thicker paint stands out the way the folds in the dress do.

9

After being left a day or so to dry, the more diluted, transparent paint is added to warm the skin of the face and hands.

10

Light opaque colors are added to areas of the skin and cardigan, laid in trails with gaps between so that the previous transparent layers show through. A few darker transparent strokes are laid across the (dry) thicker white paint of the dress. These marks help to increase the contrast, but they are also easily integrated with the paint around them as the paint spreads out thinly and a soft transition is created between the layers, a bit like glazing.

This possibility of creating subtle transitions in color and tone through techniques like glazing and scumbling (see Chapter 7) is ideal for the spontaneous painter who doesn't want to have to stop mid-flow and remix new or modified colors. Painterly tricks of this kind seem to be quintessentially Renoir: he employed every means available to steer oil paint in the direction of his vision without too much preparation or hesitation.

11

This detail shows areas heightened in color. Olive green shadows are applied to the face and hands with dilute paint—this cool color neutralizes the warm skin colors; the green mixes a little on the painting where the red-brown paint that was added to skin is still wet, but overall the effect is to increase the contrast of color in skin, and the complementaries make each other appear more vibrant.

12–13

Final emphases are added with lighter and brighter colors, laid on thickly and with a fairly dry consistency so that they stand out distinctly from what is beneath and beside them. This is much the way that an Old Master like Rubens might have added final lights on hair and skin, metal and clothing. In the seventeenth century a glaze might have been laid over these areas when dry to add luminosity and to harmonize them with the colors around. Close examination of the surface of some of Renoir's canvases suggests that he also sometimes glazed these thick lights, but not in quite the systematic way that Rubens would have. In some cases it looks like a quick wash has had the same effect. This reflects Renoir's tendency to instinctively employ all manner of means to achieve the effects he sought.

The lightest colors seen in this painting were made by adding white to lighten them, and adding a strong color to brighten them—for example, chrome yellow was added to the wooden panels behind the girl's head, viridian to the cushions on the window seat and cadmium orange to the lightest skin tones in the face.

PORTRAITS
Masterclass: Portrait of a Boy

TEMPERATURE: COOL & WARM COLORS

Renoir's paintings are characterized by a wonderful harmony of color, which he achieved through a process that began with his luminous, transparent starts and developed through his opaque, feathery brush marks and *alla prima* gestures.

Underlying this feel for color is a subtle awareness of the balance between warm and cool colors. Renoir's paintings are a study in contrasts; spontaneous and free, developing from his experimental first layers, but also with a precision and harmony achieved by years of studying, as well as an instinctual knowledge of what would work.

You will have seen "warm" and "cool" colors referred to in previous Masterclasses. The color wheel below indicates typical temperatures of colors, with orange-red at the warmest end of the scale, and green-blue at the opposite, coolest end. There are many gradations in between, and the balance of any hue can be adjusted. In the following Masterclass, a head-and-shoulders portrait of a boy is built up via a process of gradual adjustments to the temperature balance of the colors used, both in the initial glaze-like layers as well as the scumbled later stages.

warm ⟶   ⟵ cool

1

Renoir liked to begin his paintings on a smooth white canvas surface—it's worth applying several coats of gesso to your canvas and lightly sanding them smooth in between layers to get a really fine base. The painting of a boy begins by sketching out his head and shoulders in a warm red-brown dilute color, which can be smudged and rubbed out over the surface with a brush or rag until a general outline of the subject is achieved.

2

Ultramarine and lemon yellow are rubbed into the background around the figure and mixed on the canvas to create various cool green mixtures. Other dilute colors will also be applied to the face, hair, jacket and shirt. In each case the red-brown underdrawing shows through and helps to darken these colors in places, also retaining the basic form of the figure as colors are loosely applied.

3–4

A first opaque layer of skin colors is now applied to the face, painting around the initial drawing of the features. When this layer is dry (a day or two later), more ultramarine and a dark green made from ultramarine and lemon yellow are again rubbed into the background to strengthen the darks.

5

The boy's hair is darkened with a brown color made from alizarin crimson, ultramarine and lemon yellow, and this same brown is used to place the eyes and eyebrows, as well as a defining line underneath the nose. The mouth is laid in with a rich dark red.

6

Once this layer is dry, some warm, lighter skin tones are spread across the face. These colors are similar to the thin color used in the initial dilute layers, but are mixed on the palette using white, orange and a red-brown. As well as lightening the color, the thicker white also makes the paint opaque. With the thicker consistency of the paint, these areas begin to stand out more solidly and will make a good surface for subsequent transparent layers of glaze.

7

The hair is modeled with dark browns and lighter grays, and a similar treatment is applied to the clothing—some opaque mid-tone colors and some lighter edges to the shoulders and shirt collars.

8

Next, the eyes are developed, still using a warm brown from the alizarin, ultramarine and lemon. The establishment of the eyes includes a curving eyebrow, a similar mark for the eyelash and a dot for the pupil or iris. The whites of the eyes are faintly suggested with a warm gray made by neutralizing the skin color with some blue.

At this stage, the hair is glazed with a warm brown to harmonize the temperature of the colors between the face and hair—this also adds a feeling of depth or weight to the hair, making it as complex as the face has become.

9

The background greens are glazed with a cool combination of Renoir's favorite blues: cobalt and ultramarine. The yellows are left to shine through, and the jacket is covered with a warm yellow glaze.

When the painting is near completion it is worth stepping back to assess how it is working as a whole, and how best to bring it to its resolution. Here, it is a matter of softening the colors, with close attention to the temperature, while bringing out the details of the face. You can see the final painting on page 64.

While Renoir may be best known for his elaborate multifigure scenes, many of Renoir's portraits are far simpler—often just a head and shoulders against a suitable arrangement of colors in the background. These smaller portraits give you a chance to focus on the particular features of the face, to think about what you are seeing and how to translate these observations onto the canvas as simply as possible. Here, we look at some examples of the process of painting the different features: how they appear from different angles and how they are best simplified, building from the first dilute stages to the detail. Bear in mind that this is a general guide; in your studies, observation is key if you want to capture the particular expression of your subject.

EYES

Renoir would begin the features by roughly establishing skin tones and suggesting some of their overall form with light and dark tones, as well as with variation in warm and cool skin colors.

The eye viewed straight on (top row) is roughly symmetrical and can be defined at the juice stage with a few simple marks. Look for the shape of the eyebrow and the shadow where it joins the nose; the upper eyelid with a crease at the top and an eyelash at the outer corner; the round shape of the iris; the rim of the lower lid, which tends to catch light and thus can be used to define the lower edge of the eye; and finally the shadow of the lower lid.

Seen from the side, or profile view, the eye is like a v on its side with the same sequence of landmarks (middle row). Certain parts of it, like the eyebrow and the lids with their shadows, will be foreshortened.

At three-quarters (bottom row) the view of the eye is not symmetrical— if you imagine a central line down the middle of the eye, one half will be foreshortened, or compressed, and the overall shape is now fish-shaped rather than almond.

When the first thinly-painted impression is dry, the eyes are developed using dark lines and shapes applied with a sable brush. At this point, the paint is still thinned with linseed oil and turps so that these definitions are subtly brought out with slightly stronger darks, and gently graded from one layer to the next.

The third layer consists of thicker, drier paint. Black is used to strengthen the darkest points of the eyebrow and eyelash (thicker and stronger in the center of the arches of the eyelid to bring this part forward). Black is also used for the pupil and cobalt blue for the color of the iris—obviously this color will depend on your subject. The color is strongest in the lower part of the iris and lightened with white. The whites of the eye are also mainly visible in lower areas, where they are not so shaded by the upper eyelid, and so should be brighter here. Mid- and light warm skin tones are used on the top lid and the rim of lower lid, and red marks are made to the inside corner of the eye and lashes.

The final layer consists of those last marks of emphasis and detail: the hairs of the eyebrow, a catchlight in the eye and so on. Be careful not to invent at this stage, though: these studies should help you learn to look and record what you see, rather than what you expect to see.

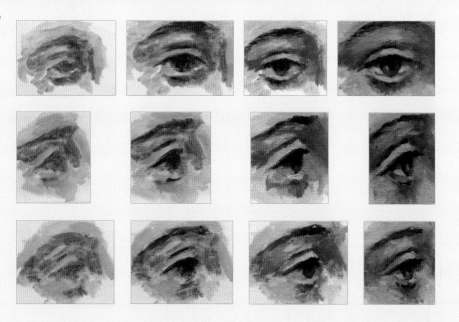

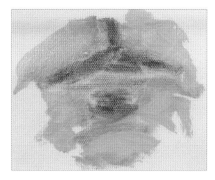
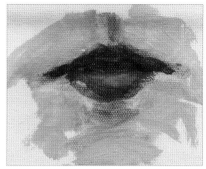
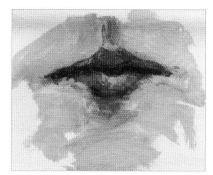

MOUTHS

Like the eyes, the mouth has a different appearance according to the angle at which it is viewed. Seen straight on (top row), the combination of a thin, dark upper lip and a thick, short and lighter lower lip has a symmetrical arrangement. In profile (second row) those elements, like the eye, roughly form the shape of a v on its side, with the angle of the upper lip giving a shadow while the lower lip curves out to catch some light, which is simply indicated by a dab of the color that was used for the skin. In the three-quarter view, the mouth may be seen as a combination of elements of the straight-on and profile view. The nearest half comprises a long upper lip that tapers down to the corner of the mouth, and the lower lip that doesn't quite meet the corner. The central section is indicated by a short horizontal line, beyond which the far half of the mouth is compressed or foreshortened as it curves around the face.

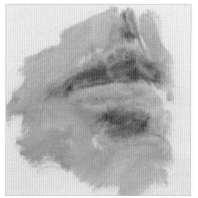

NOSES

The eyes and mouth require particular attention, as these are the most expressive features of the face. They are mobile and essential to the character and emotion of the portrait. Other features like noses and chins should not be neglected, however. These features also vary widely from person to person and can often be just as important in adding to a sense of character or personality. Because they don't move in the same expressive way that eyes and mouths do, the key thing here will be accurately modeling their forms and understanding their shapes from different viewpoints.

The tip of nose is a round shape, flanked by the wings of the nostrils, connected to a long bony plane that connects at the top to the ridge of the eyebrows.

In the illustration below left, the symmetrical, straight-on view (on the right) is modeled with darker planes at either side that are narrow at the bridge of the nose, widening where they descend into the wings of the nostrils. A darker, curved plane is placed under the tip of the nose, and into this the dark openings of the nostrils are indicated. These same elements are also part of the modeling of the three-quarter view (on the left), but this time only one shaded side of the nose is visible, as well as the front plane. A thin dark line defines the far edge of the front plane, hinting the beginning of the plane on the opposite side of the nose.

At the next stage (below right), thicker layers of opaque colors are applied. The marks are placed to reinforce the basic form of the nose, as well as to refine some of the subtle details—such as the way the front plane is narrowest at the bridge, widening in the center and narrowing again just before the tip. Remember that all noses are different—this effect may be less noticeable in a straighter nose and more emphatic in a bonier, bumpier nose, for example.

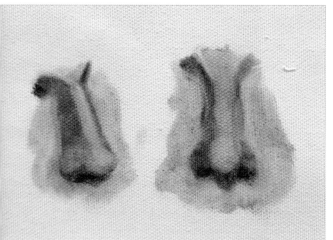
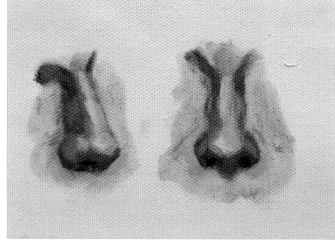

Observation will help you to become more aware of the effects of light and shadows on different nose shapes—and this will help you to paint not a general idea of a nose, but a nose specific to your subject.

As the nose develops, the shadow colors are lightened and cooled, and a warm mid-tone shadow under the tip forms part of the spherical modeling of this form. An extra line of light is dragged down one edge of the front of the nose and placed as the lightest point on the rounded tip. Note that the wings of the nostrils are light, but not as light as the front and tip, and perhaps a little cooler. The openings of the nostrils are strengthened with a warm dark mark. Be careful not to overemphasize these marks—although they need to be indicated, they really say nothing about the form of the nose, and if they are too strong they will stand out and undermine the modeling that has been created through light and shade and cool and warm colors.

CHINS

A chin is basically a hemispherical form that may be squarer or rounder, longer or shorter according to your subject. Keeping in mind the idea of a central line dividing the face will help when modeling the form of the chin according to various different orientations.

Similar steps have been taken with the two views of the hemispherical chin as with the nose: the round form of this feature is modeled from above by the curved notch below the lower lip, and from below by the round outline of the bottom of the chin (below left). These forms are made more substantial and distinct by building up the warm and cool, and gradually lighter and thicker colors that end with a spot of very light paint toward the top of one side (below right) where the light falls, with a corresponding warm shadow on the opposite lower side. These final emphases all work to sculpt the three-dimensional form of the chin.

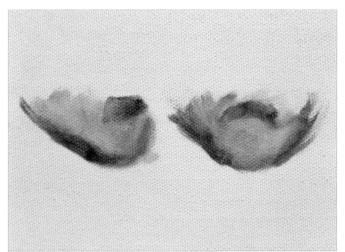

PORTRAITS
Masterclass: Portrait of a Girl

ADDING DETAILS

This Masterclass will guide you through the whole process of painting a simple head-and-shoulders portrait, from the first transparent juice layers to the particular details and features that are brought out toward the end of the painting.

1–2

The shape of the girl's hair is sketched out in a thin brown color. The face is also mapped out, with some variation in the strength of the color or thickness of paint so that there is some suggestion of the modeling of the face.

3

After 15 minutes by the heater, this first thin layer is dry. Paint thinned with turps and linseed oil is added to the background areas and clothing to block in the composition, and the hair color is now built up more strongly.

This approach to painting the face, where each area is seen as a discrete shape to be first loosely blocked in, then refined and built up, is well worth trying. Renoir's shapes would probably have been even vaguer than mine are, giving him a lot of freedom to adapt as he progressed. The point, however, is that faces are challenging subjects and it is tempting to start by drawing and painting specific small features, and get stuck on these without ever having a clear vision of the whole face and the totality of the subject. By contrast, with this approach you are working toward ever more definite shapes, using both soft and defined edges, culminating with the final emphasis and the details of the features. This tends to help one to do less and, therefore, produce stronger images.

4

A warm pink skin mid-tone is applied to the cheeks and the areas around the eyes. If you look at a face it is often in these places that the skin has a warm or ruddy complexion. A lighter and more colorful yellow ocher hair color is also applied. The paint at this stage is still fairly thin and well spread out; still mapping out the key areas of tone and hue.

5

A warm brown is applied with a sable brush to begin to define the lines of the eyes, nose and mouth.

6

The mouth has a thicker red color added to it and the eyes are developed with the details of the pupils, iris and whites. Using thinner paint allows these features to be rendered with subtlety. When the thicker opaque paint is applied at the next stage it will only be necessary to add a small amount to bring them out.

7

After being left to dry for a few days, the painting is ready for the next stages. A warm olive green is applied thinly, or scumbled, across shadow areas. This heightens the overall color of the face and also improves temperature balance; with all those reds, the face was too hot. This is a quick and approximate task that adds depth and weight to the face.

8

Thin trails of lighter cream and a warm white color are dragged across the skin areas following some of the contours of the forehead and the cheeks. These touches both stand out as highlights and slightly merge with (or emerge from) the thinner layer below. The natural translucency of skin is well emulated by this effect.

9

The mouth and eyes are painted alla prima *with more substantial quantities of paint, somewhat following the basic design laid out in the underpainting but worked and reworked with colors mixing on the surface of the painting. As ever, this kind of emphasis is held together and unified by the luminous layer of color beneath.*

In the previous three stages, a variety of techniques has been used, including glazing (a transparent layer over dry paint), scumbling (a thin opaque layer spread out over dry surface) and alla prima. *This is typical of Renoir's mixed approach, exploiting all the different ways in which oil paint can be handled— but they do need to be approached with a certain amount of discipline, or the techniques will not have the desired effect. For example, glazing and scumbling only work over a dry surface, using quite small quantities of paint, while* alla prima *painting only really works if sufficient quantities of paint are boldly pitched into a kind of battle for clarity and subtlety.*

10

Finally, one more layer of mixed tints is applied using fairly small marks. These extend the range of pinks, yellows and oranges in the light areas, and the cool blues and greens in the shadows. Though colorful, the hues balance each other so that the overall effect is not too garish.

PORTRAITS
Exercises

1 SELF-PORTRAIT PRACTICE

For many artists one of the hardest things about portraiture is the pressure of working with a live model. They may distract you by talking, figeting and wanting to see your composition—or you may simply become overly aware of time. All these distractions will ultimately detract from the painting, by making you hurry or lose your focus. The best way to overcome these obstacles is, of course, practice. Before asking friends and family to sit for their portraits, then, set up a mirror on a second easel (or anywhere that it can be propped up) and first experiment with the technique with a self-portrait. Doing this will give you a chance to become more confident in your portraiture. You can stop and start the painting at your leisure, and, when the time comes, you will be able to arrange the several sittings with your model with a far better idea of how long each stage will take and how long will be needed in between.

This exercise may seem simple, but I can't stress enough how useful it will be to developing your confidence with the medium in a portrait scenario.

2 SIMPLE FEATURES

Set up two mirrors on two easels, or propped up however you can around your workspace, to allow you to see your own features from different angles and viewpoints. As with the first exercise, it will be worth practicing on your own until you have built up your confidence, but if you can find a patient model with whom you feel comfortable that will certainly make this exercise easier.

Mix a simple three-color palette with a light, a dark and a neutral tone. Using a reasonably large brush (size 10 square, for example) make small studies of your features from the

different angles. Follow the process outlined on pages 68–71, beginning with thin diluted paint and a rough sketch, to thicker layers, and opaque details.

Attempt to keep your studies as simple as possible, choosing marks with care and painting just what you see. Limiting your palette to three colors also gives you a good opportunity to see how much depth and variety is possible just by working through the process of building up layers, modulating the consistency of the paint and using different brush techniques.

CHAPTER 5: FIGURE GROUPS

Renoir was clearly a sociable animal, and his desire to paint happy paintings was satisfied in the compositions that featured his friends at leisure. He frequented particular dance venues and cafés, and, with the typical Impressionist philosophy, he sought to depict the everyday world around him. He tended to choose the more timeless activities of eating, drinking and dancing for his themes—though while the subjects may have been traditional, his treatments of them were highly modern. You can observe in Renoir's multifigure compositions the Impressionist idiom of loose brushwork and heightened colors and the fascination with the quality of the light, as well as in his typical subject matter of friends and working-class people enjoying themselves. "Nature leads the artist into loneliness," he said, explaining his rejection of the landscape subject, "I want to remain among people."

A composition containing several figures can be an intimidating prospect for any artist, so this chapter explores several different ways in which you can approach a multifigure painting. We begin by looking at approaches that diverge from Renoir's own technique, but which will help you get a feel for scale and perspective; then, returning to the familiar process of building the composition up in a series of layers, a Masterclass will take you through the particular challenge of balancing both foreground and background elements in a complex composition. Finally we will take on the biggest challenge—a *plein air* multifigure composition, executed loosely and with an eye to the key concerns of the Impressionists.

FIGURE GROUPS
Approaching the Composition

In his extraordinary paintings of groups, it appeared that Renoir followed the process of building up layers from an initial diluted juice layer to thicker paint and careful detail. In this way the painting developed organically, each part and each element in harmony with the rest, while leaving Renoir free to adapt the composition as he saw fit—the striped orange awning at the top of the *Luncheon of the Boating Party* (see page 29) is one such detail that was a late addition to the canvas. Essentially, a multifigure composition may be approached in just the same way as a landscape or portrait painting (or perhaps a combination of the two).

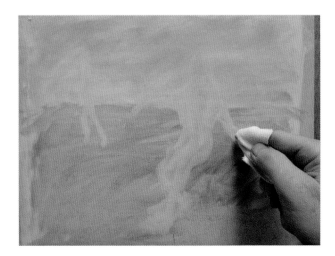

It can, however, be easy for the inexperienced painter to be overwhelmed by the huge amount of detail that needs to go into the composition. The Masterclasses that follow later in this chapter apply Renoir's method of building the composition gradually from a juice layer, but here we will look at a some alternative approaches that hopefully will help to ease you into the process. I recommend taking the figures that you will add to the scene from a number of different photographs, thinking about how their different poses will work in the composition as a whole.

APPROACH 1:
NEAR & FAR ALL AT ONCE

This approach begins with a simple background, blocked in but still wet. The negative shapes of your figures are now wiped out of the background paint using a clean rag (top). If you struggle with perspective, keeping heads on a similar level can help. Wiping out the shape of the figure is an excellent way of seeing the overall form and not getting lost in details, and because the background—however rudimentary—is also already painted, neither are you initially fighting against the white of the canvas.

Your "ghost" figures can now be blocked in with some dilute colors, which mix a little with the background paint (middle). The figures gradually begin to emerge, while naturally remaining part of their surroundings.

The painting will now need to be left to dry for a day, after which the process may be continued by adding some extra figures (bottom). Here, I added a larger foreground figure and a smaller figure in the background. These two were painted with thinned oils straight over the background colors and parts of the existing figures as well. When figures overlap like this, the effect of distance and foreground seems more natural and authentic—in real life, people aren't normally lined up, nicely regimented and tidy. The background colors showing through the new figures helps to absorb them into their surroundings and adds depth and complexity to the colors on the figures.

The foreground figures are now worked on further, much in the same way as we've seen in the previous chapters of landscape and portrait paintings (top). Opaque layers of color and contrast are gradually built up in the foreground figures, helping these figures to stand out more than the fainter ones behind. More detail is now also added in the background; more contrast and texture in the foreground area to bring this forward. Work on the sky and grass also helps to bring the figures together so that they seem to occupy the same space.

The opaque work continues with the largest, foremost figure being worked on with more detail and in thicker paint, and on the second-largest figure as well (bottom). The important thing to assess here is how much to do to the relatively distant figures. As the nearer figures become stronger, those in the background may begin to appear insufficiently painted and will need more attention. The best way to judge the balancing of different parts of the painting is by standing back from your work so that you can take in the whole effect. Ideally, you will develop a figure or some of the background, not because you can, but because it is needed in order for that element to fulfill its role in the composition as a whole, for example to stand out because it is near, or important; or to recede for the opposite reasons.

FIGURE GROUPS
Approaching the Composition

APPROACH 2:
WORKING FROM THE BACK TO THE FRONT

The challenge of getting the perspective right can be one of the hardest parts of a multifigure painting, so this example offers another approach: starting from the smallest figures at the back, you can then work through the medium-sized figures that are nearer, to the largest figures in the foreground. The relative sizes of your figures will determine the perceived depth of the scene, making this excellent practice for working with perspective. This approach of working forward from the figures farthest back can be usefully implemented even if your figures are all closely grouped, with little distance between them.

To begin, another simple background is laid out in thinned paint to suggest sky and grass and the shapes of two small figures are wiped out near the horizon and then blocked in simply with dilute colors (top left).

Working toward the foreground, two figures of medium size are added in the same way: first wiped out (top right), and then blocked in (bottom left). These are able to overlap and obscure parts of the smaller figures behind, helping to create a natural arrangement of figures in space.

The process continues with larger foreground figures being added (bottom right, opposite left). In each case, heads are kept on a similar level, while feet appear progressively lower on the canvas, and in the last cases cropped at the bottom.

Next, the colors of the surrounding sky and grass are strengthened with thicker paint, and the the two foreground figures are worked on (opposite right). Once these are more established, a little more can be done to the middle-distance and background figures, with the expectation that the nearest figures will ultimately have more attention and more paint used on them so that they stand out the most.

DRAWING THE COMPOSITION

In most of Renoir's paintings, the composition appears to have been developed during the very early stages of the painting, when he exploited the tendency of diluted transparent paint to suggest form, atmosphere and even the color scheme. Renoir's *Luncheon of the Boating Party*, which we have already seen on pages 28–29, is an example of an extremely complex composition that Renoir seems to have created without the help of previously made studies or an underdrawing.

This is not to say that you shouldn't make any sketches, though. It should be remembered that Renoir had studied and been practicing his craft for many years. Sketches, both of individual figures and your vision for the composition as a whole, will help you to clarify your ideas as well as giving you something to refer back to as the painting progresses.

Renoir did make a number of pencil drawings and studies on tracing paper, which relate to particular paintings. These line drawings show a definite vision in terms of the composing of the several figures featured. If you choose to make studies before beginning with oil paints, try to keep your drawings simple and loose—by keeping only the essential qualities of what you intend to convey, your painting has room to develop in the more natural, organic way characteristic of the Impressionist approach.

FIGURE GROUPS
Masterclass: Two Girls in the Garden

FIGURES & BACKGROUND

In contrast to the simple head-and-shoulders portrait, when Renoir painted his friends and family in social groups, out in the open air, he was combining several different elements all in one picture—figure, landscape and sometimes still life. These different parts of the painting needed to work together, to be unified in some way and carefully balanced, so that one part of the image didn't overwhelm the rest.

Renoir loved detail in his paintings, and this is part of his popular appeal. This Masterclass looks at how to manage this detail when you are working on a fairly complex composition. Initially, the painting focuses on two figures, one of which is developed while the background is kept loose and indefinite. Once the background is developed further, it becomes necessary to consider what needs to be done to the figure to ensure that it maintains its importance in the scene.

1

The scene, based on two girls standing in a garden, is sketched out in blues, with a larger foreground figure in profile and a smaller figure raised on a bridge in the background. Some colors are added to the figures and their clothing.

This layer is left to dry.

2

Once dry, yellows and greens are applied thinly and quite roughly to the background, developing the blues and making the image more colorful. Some greens and yellows are allowed to spill into the figures in order to tint the skin and clothing.

3

The figures are now worked on with thicker, more opaque paint, and as a result the girl in front stands out particularly strongly. The opaque paint is applied loosely, always leaving gaps for the lower layers to be visible and affect the surface appearance.

4

A detail shows how the faces and the rest of the figures have been developed further. Their features are roughly indicated and more color added to clothing and hair. All this detail and emphasis gives them a more substantial quality, while the background remains blurred as if out of focus.

5

Moving onto the background, the next step is to strengthen some of the dark areas of the trees and foliage. A viridian green, neutralized and darkened with a little alizarin crimson, is applied loosely in a wash to the yellow and green surroundings. The heightened contrast between colors makes the background stronger but also actually brings the figure of the girl out even more.

6

Next, some of the different greens and colorful flowers are laid on top of the thinner layer, and the garden begins to become more vivid and defined.

7

Here we can see the whole composition. A common feature of Renoir's landscapes was the presence of one or more figures lost in a swarm of brush marks, texture and color. In later figure compositions he experimented with the degree to which figures and their settings are defined.

PLEIN AIR GROUPS

The new vision in painting favored by the Impressionists and their contemporaries was often to be found in natural phenomena—early morning or late evening light, snow and smoggy weather conditions. They were curious about the actual experience of a moment—reality as it appeared to the eye and the mind, rather than as it appeared in the precise reproduction of a camera, or even of the paintings of the past. What we experience is, in fact, often much more of a jumble than we register—not every detail of a scene will be in focus—and what we see is often a great blur of color and light. Different weather and light conditions each brought a different kind of experience for the Impressionists to record.

This effect can be particularly useful when working on what would be a fairly complex group scene. You don't need to record every fine detail to effectively convey a group—and sometimes it is best not to. This Masterclass combines a multifigure composition with Impressionist concerns; in particular the fall of sunlight through a canopy of leaves, giving a broken, mosaic-like quality to the light, which renders forms in a fragmented, confused way—in other words, perfect for the short, discrete Impressionist *tache*. Hopefully this Masterclass will also demonstrate how easy it is to build up a fair multifigure composition from a rough juice sketch.

1

Cobalt blue, thinned with a mixture of two parts turps to one part linseed oil, is used to sketch out the figures in the scene, the bench on which they sit and the pattern of their shadows. This particular color was chosen to emulate Renoir's interest in blue shadows and build a painting of dappled light around them.

2

Most of the white canvas is covered in a similar way with some pink hues for the ground and some yellows and greens for the distant park. It is useful to block in the canvas at an early stage, so that you can work it up at the same time as the figures, which both helps you to work on the canvas as a whole—therefore keeping the composition unified—and should prevent you from becoming overly focused on particular details too early.

3

Different shades of blue are added to certain parts of the figures, indicating differences in their clothing. Red is applied to hair, and some more pinks are painted on and then rubbed into the canvas with a clean rag.

4

Orange skin colors are now applied to the dry thin first layer. These stand out particularly well against their opposite blues. The very lightest skin tones are laid on thickly so that they are raised on the surface of the painting.

5

A brown wash is spread, sometimes stabbed on, across the foreground figures, the bench and their shadows. The wash produces several effects: it darkens the figures, which are anyway silhouetted, contre-jour. *It also softens the contrasts between all the various colors that have been used on the figures, but without obliterating their differences in color, texture and tone. Finally, it adjusts the warm/cool balance wholesale, and creates a new degree of depth to the image; particularly a depth of color between the complementary opposites of blue and orange (this brown being essentially a dark, dull orange).*

6

Warm pale pinks are applied opaquely to the ground areas and in between the shadows. The paint is applied by holding the very end of the long brush handle, so that a stabbing stroke can be applied. This is helpful because as more paint lands on the canvas with limited mixing, it suggests the pattern of dappled light and it delays the definition of any of the forms.

7

More pinks are applied to the floor with this stabbing mark. The inevitable mixing of wet-on-wet oil paint is helpful here, as the subject is shadows with soft edges: all the subtle mixes possible from the shadow blues and the orange-pinks are created on the painting's surface, and so out of two bright opposites various muted neutrals are generated. However, as with all alla prima oil painting, it is important to be aware of what is on the tip of your brush as you apply paint. Where these mixtures are created on the painting, your brush will also have picked them up and they may be usefully applied somewhere else, if desired. If, however, you decide that sharp, fresh colors are needed at the next step, you should wipe the brush and be sure of picking up

a clean mixture. It is tempting to outline forms and delineate them once and for all, but try to resist this and allow the painting to gradually evolve. Something that attracted the Impressionists to the effects of sunlight and weather was the fact that solid forms were often dissolved or softened and this was the vision they wanted to paint—one where painterly marks were as evident to the viewer as the illusion of the subject itself. They took pleasure in the medium as well as in the subject.

8

The bench becomes a bit more solid and definite with the use of thin darks and lighter colorful paint. I gradually work toward the figures using broken marks. The clothing, heads and arms are developed, but it is good to notice and take stock of the ways in which the defining bench and ground help the people to emerge. This should be kept in mind so that when they are being refined and brought out, it can be done in the most economical way—by doing less.

9

A warm orange color is applied to faces, arms and hands. This has a big impact on the whole painting: the people come together better now that they have developed heads, and the fact that the major color relationships are blue and orange means the balance has been restated and colors harmonize overall. Lighter, thicker highlights are applied to faces and hands—generally these marks are still made as short taches, or stabbed on to maintain the dappled or mosaic effect.

FIGURE GROUPS
Masterclass: Figures on a Bench

COLOR IN SHADOWS

Impressionism was a revolution in painting—it presented a new way of seeing the world, notably the outdoor world. Toward the end of the nineteenth century, scientists were developing new ideas and theories about color, and these in turn influenced artists such as Renoir. An understanding of complementary effects—the fact that opposite colors placed side by side excite each other, making each other stand out all the more boldly, was put to use in an effort to create more vibrant paintings. Renoir often used bright blue in his shadows as a complementary opposite to the orange/pink ground on which the light and shadows fell. He would apparently seek out locations where the shadows appeared to be blue and organize his painting around this effect. In this Masterclass the figures seated on a Paris park bench cast a long bluish shadow shape on the foreground area.

1

The picture is sketched out in dilute blue paint, thinned with turps and linseed oil, on a smooth white canvas surface. Figures The ground is blocked in with a pale pink.

2

Both figures and background are blocked in using two colors for each area; a dark and muted version and a lighter, brighter version of each color.

3

When the painting is dry, a thin sable brush is used to apply fine lines to indicate the features on the faces of the figures using a brown mixture made from the transparent pigments of alizarin crimson, ultramarine and lemon yellow. Mouths are also painted in using a warm red made from cadmium orange and alizarin.

4

A stiff hog hair brush is used to build up patterns small brushstrokes in different parts of the painting. The Impressionist *tache* was a short substantial brushstroke that deposited a clear mark on the surface of the painting, leaving it to stand out and create a more textured and vibrant effect. This is what we are aiming for here.

5

The painting is developed further with more marks and colors distributed around the composition.

6

As the color develops in other parts of the picture, the different blues in the shadow shapes are also elaborated upon.

FIGURE GROUPS
Exercises

1 WORKING FROM PHOTOGRAPHS

When you are building up your experience of working with figure groups it can be a good idea to start with photographs. Then you don't have to worry about your models moving around or getting bored, and there isn't such a pressure of time—although it is still worth working quickly.

Take some photographs of friends or family outdoors, ideally busy in some social activity; eating, picnicking or dancing. It can be helpful if these pictures are slightly blurred so that you have just the basic forms and colors of your subjects to work from—you can either do this at the time of shooting or later using computer software. If you do the former, take another photo that is in focus at the same time. Then follow the stages demonstrated in this chapter using the modified photos for reference, building up from a loose, thin, transparent background, and thinking about your color choices, marks and emphases as you work through the stages of opaque paint. Pay particular attention to the quality of the light at this stage, how it falls on your subjects and its color.

A further step would be to refer to the original in-focus photograph at the end of the painting when you are ready to add some extra detail or emphasis. For this stage, you may want to photograph or sketch some individual character studies to help you see their expression or pose more clearly. It is important that what you do at this stage must be in-keeping with what has already been built up, so do it with either dilute paint or a slightly-too-large brush.

2 ADDING FIGURES ORGANICALLY

Working either from life or from photographs, build up a crowd of figures in an outdoor setting. Allow the composition to develop organically by adding one or two figures at a time, and then leaving the painting to dry. It can be interesting to try this exercise on an old painting, where the existing textures and color are helpful in absorbing the new figures and suggesting the background and surroundings (top).

Add your figures instinctively and make them different sizes. Keeping the heads on a similar level will help with the scale, and you should achieve a sense depth and perspective (middle). Try overlapping figures, and having the largest, nearest figures cropped out of the frame in places (bottom). A horizon can also be helpful. You will begin to get a feel for composing groups of figures and exercise your own instincts for creating crowds. Adding figures gradually, leaving the painting to dry and allowing yourself time to enter into what's developing in the painting is a good way of experiencing something of the instinctive approach to an evolving composition that artists like Renoir would take.

When a few figures have been added and some work done to the background—some shadows on the ground or some receding trees to help with the perspective, for instance—something begins to happen between the figures. A little like characters in a novel, they start to relate to each other, you begin to perceive relationships forming, and by studying this emerging dialog it's possible to see what you should do next, for example where to add figures, what size or color to make them and so on.

Renoir would work in a similar way, using particular outdoor venues and recreating from memory and with the help of models scenes that he often witnessed in these favorite haunts.

CHAPTER 6: RENOIR & STILL LIFE

Renoir explained that he sometimes resorted to painting flowers in order to rest his brain. He certainly used the subject to explore some of his later warm red palettes, and in fact he seemed to execute his still life paintings with tremendous energy and a full *alla prima* virtuoso touch. Although his subject matter of fruits and flowers might be rather traditional, his painting style was not. Still-life compositions gave him the chance to practice his avant garde techniques without fear of offending his subjects—who often complained that the Impressionist technique he painted their portraits with was unflattering.

As well as being easier subjects to tackle, flowers and fruit offered Renoir bright colors and textures to explore, and he clearly selected the natural objects for these qualities. A particularly rich and succulent example, *Fruits of the Midi* (1881), combines the deep purples of eggplant with the bright yellows of lemons and the reds of pimentos. The way in which these once living subjects change and decay quickly holds a further attraction for the *alla prima* painter: the imperative to capture their brief glory is an incentive to work quickly and boldly. The French for "still life" is *"nature morte,"* or "dead nature." In Renoir's still lifes, however, everything he does with color, brushwork and definition, brings his subject matter to life.

RENOIR & STILL LIFE
Experiments in Still Life

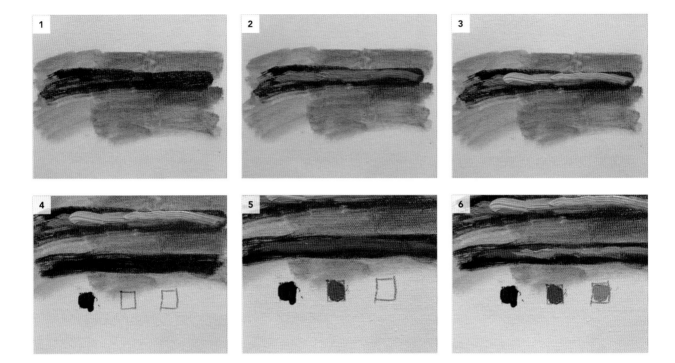

Examination of Renoir's paintings of fruit and flowers and still life objects reveals that he developed these paintings according to the familiar stages of thinned luminous paint beneath thicker opaque brush marks with which he approached his other subjects.

The key difference between Renoir's approach to still-life paintings and other subjects is that he felt much more free to be experimental, to take risks without worrying about losing the picture. His instinctive and energetic painterly descriptions of his subjects in oils offer a fantastic lesson in the art of drawing with paint. You should follow this approach and see it as an opportunity to practice new methods, try out new techniques and explore different color combinations.

The illustrations on these pages demonstrate the kind of experiments you should try for yourself, using different types of brushes, consistencies, marks and so on. It is worthwhile keeping a sketchbook or making a series of small swatches, perhaps on offcuts of canvas, where you can save the results of your experiments and return to them for reference and inspiration. Remember to note down what you did!

1–3: Cobalt blue and alizarin crimson are thinned with a mixture of turps and linseed oil to make Renoir's thin "juice." The diluted paints are then spread on a white canvas and allowed to mix in the middle.

A dark opaque mixture of the two colors is dragged over the translucent juice layer, allowed to blend in some places and floated in others. A lighter mid-tone consisting of the two colors plus white is floated onto the dark line. To successfully float a layer, the paint needs to be in sufficient quantity so as to lie on the wet surface without the brush picking up the existing wet layer.

A final layer of lightest (and thickest) paint is floated over this. To do this, the brush is held almost parallel to the surface of the canvas.

4–6: The process is repeated, this time using a redder mixture. Again, I work from dark to light, increasing the quantity of the paint with each new wet layer.

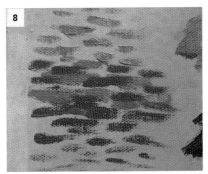

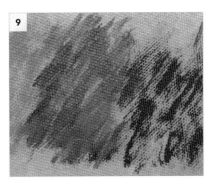

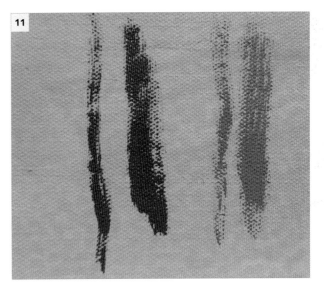

7: Cobalt blue and alizarin crimson are thinned with linseed oil and turps into a sort of glaze and spread across a dry blue surface. Some paint is then dabbed off with a rag.

8: Thick, light mixtures of pink and blue are made by adding white to alizarin crimson and cobalt blue. Short, Impressionist *tache* marks are made, leaving gaps in between and growing denser toward where the two colors meet in the middle.

9: Light opaque mixtures are scumbled over a blue ground, leaving gaps that allow the color beneath to show through.

10. The two colors used in these experiments: cobalt blue and alizarin crimson. The pigments are diluted with turps and linseed oil, spread out over the canvas and allowed to mix in the middle.

11. Light mixtures of the two colors are dry-brushed across a yellow surface. The brush is cleaned in turps and then dried before oil paint is picked up.

RENOIR & STILL LIFE
Masterclass: Flowers in a Vase

PAINT HANDLING IN STILL LIFE

Still lifes offer a good opportunity to choose objects with different textures and really concentrate on using the paint in a way that emulates their particular qualities. This Masterclass takes you through the process with particular emphasis on the handling of the paint in terms of both consistency and mark-making. The intention is to find the marks that best capture the esseence of the jug of flowers.

1

The whole still-life arrangement of flowers is sketched out in a dilute red color. The variation in the strength of the solution gives a tonal range to the picture and helps to model the forms.

2

Some of the main colors are blocked in; the paint is still relatively thin so that colors will retain a luminous quality from the white ground of the primed canvas.

The paint is applied in short, broken brush marks so that the layers and colors beneath show through in the gaps between the marks. This allows the transparent colors to shine through and illuminate the whole image. It also helps to create a more subtle and even delicate quality to the leaves and petals. The vase is painted in a similarly broken manner, so the original red layer shows through here as well and helps to hold the painting together as more colors are applied.

3

The next stage is a shift into opaque colors. You will find that some pigments are more opaque than others—in this case the opacity is created partly by the presence of the more opaque white pigment in the lighter mixtures and also simply because the paint is being applied more thickly.

A hog hair brush is held almost parallel to the canvas and a quantity of light-colored paint is placed onto the petals of an orange flower. The brush marks are all placed in different directions in an attempt to capture something of the structure and pattern of the flower. In this detail you can see how the edges of the flowers and the leaves are created, and how in many places they are not at all sharply defined. Sometimes an edge is defined by the lighter opaque background color; in other places the layers of red underpainting, thin petal color and finally thicker pale petal marks combine to give a varied and soft effect where the layers merge.

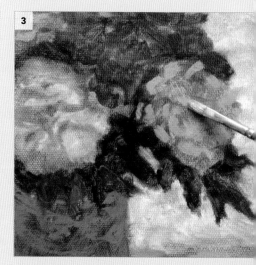

4

A smaller, square-headed brush is turned on its side in order to generate a varied brush mark that reflects the tapered shape of the outer petals. You can see in this detail how the lighter paint being applied now is thicker than what was used on the layers beneath.

5

Here you can see the two colors that, combined, give solidity and contrast in the leaves. The darker green is applied first, describing the overall shape of each leaf, then the lighter color is laid into this base with a wavy brushstroke reflecting the finger-like form of the leaf tips. Depending on the degree to which the lighter color is pressed into the dark or alternatively floated on its surface, a soft or sharp edge is created between the light and dark areas.

6

A yellow flower has been built up further in a similar way to the others, with thicker, lighter color and further variations in the shadow colors of the petals. A basic contrast is established between thin receding paint and thick emerging colors—this reflects the structure of the flower head, with the tips of petals standing out from the base of the flower through impasto marks on a stained canvas surface.

7

In this more finished painting, the busy mosaic mark of the flowers is echoed and repeated in the treatment of the background, and this adds life and vitality to the whole composition.

RENOIR & STILL LIFE
Masterclass: Yellow Roses

COLOR & STILL LIFE

Renoir was at his most experimental in his still-life paintings, and you should try to adopt this mindset in your own work. See still life as the subject where you can push techniques, colors and all aspects of your painting further than you would in portraiture or landscape, and don't worry about losing the picture—the idea is to find out what works. The things you learn through making still lifes can be applied to your more formal work.

Rather than rushing to get out all your pigments, however, remember that the beautiful harmony of color in Renoir's still-life paintings often comes from his use of closely related sets of colors that have been allowed to mix at the early dilute stage of the painting. As we saw earlier, he used this stage of the painting to find the form it would later take. Colors would often be put down quickly and almost at random until the idea began to take shape. He would then build up from here in thicker, more opaque layers, and add details.

It can be helpful to identify some simple sets of colors that work together well, and then restrict your palette to these for most of the painting. In the following Masterclass I used a palette of six pre-mixed colors (below left) mixed from chrome yellow, Naples yellow, viridian green, alizarin crimson and white. New colors will be generated as the painting progresses, but because they will have been mixed from these six, they will bear family resemblances to each other and the end result will have a harmony to it, instead of appearing busy or clashing.

1

The composition is sketched out in a gestural way to capture a sense of movement in the bunch of roses and the palm leaves behind them. The leaves are painted in dilute colors based on viridian green, neutralized and darkened with alizarin crimson, and the flower shapes are blocked in with chrome yellow.

This dilute mix of colors, thinned with turps and linseed oil, blends easily when these shapes overlap as they are loosely placed on the canvas. When some of the green is picked up by the yellow, a perfect cool shadow color is generated for the petals. This is just the kind of happy accident you should be on the lookout for, not just in still lifes but always—let the painting do some of the work for you!

2

A brown background is also blocked in so that the white of the canvas can be subdued and the relationships between the new colors will be seen more clearly. Note, though, how the flowers and leaves were painted directly onto the white. The bright white coming through from behind gives a luminosity to the subject that will shine through these thinly applied layers.

When you come to apply more opaque paint, it will be worth considering the kinds of marks you use in order to ensure that this first transparent layer still comes through, adding depth and helping to unify during the later stages of the painting.

3

A detail shows how the first opaque colors are applied to the petals. As the colors of the transparent layer have a luminous effect, the opaque colors should complement this. In other words, they will need to be mixed from vibrant sources such as chrome yellow and viridian.

4

A different, greener mixture of chrome yellow and viridian is also used for the leaves, the forms of which begin to be defined. As these colors are all quite cool, a warm color is mixed from chrome yellow and brown. This is applied to the flowers where they are shadowed, and balances the temperature a little.

5

Much as Renoir might have done at this early stage of the process, the darks are now increased to full strength and mid-tones worked up as well.

6

It is also worth making the background more opaque at this point, as it helps to bring the subject forward.

7

Another detail now shows the range of color and paint handling. There should still be areas of thinner luminous color showing through the gaps in the thicker opaque marks. The opaque mixtures floated on top need to be heightened in color in the lightest areas in order to stand out brightly against the dilute washes in the gaps. These lighter colors are painted both thickly and descriptively—finer observations, such as the delicate edges of petals or the ribbing of the leaves, have been made by painting lighter wet color into mid-toned still-wet paint.

8

As more warm colors are applied to the flowers the temperature of the colors in the leaves seem relatively cool. Standing back from your painting will help you to see the overall temperature more easily. Here, a balance is struck by noticing and adding in the warm browns along the edges of the leaves.

RENOIR & STILL LIFE
Alla Prima & *Still Life*

There are two distinct factors that can each inform and inspire your *alla prima* approach. The diluted juice underlayer with which Renoir began his paintings, and which we in turn are emulating, needs heightened color in the subsequent opaque layers. As the paint builds up, there is a necessity to float greater quantities each time in order to make an impact. Gradually this becomes almost an exercise in sculpting the paint.

Secondly, as you will know if you've tried painting *en plein air*, your handling of the paint can be inspired by the subject

itself. Take a while with your subject to really observe its qualities; not only color and texture, but whether it is shiny or luminous or dull, thin and fragile or solid and heavy, and so on. How can you best sum up these qualities in paint?

Renoir's instinctive and spontaneous approach is nicely captured in the following comment, "I am a little cork which has fallen into the water, carried away by the current." The following examples explore how the subject and necessities of the form inspire the approach you might take.

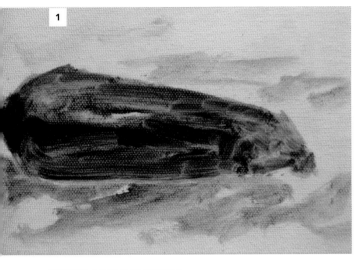

EGGPLANT (TEXTURE)

1

The rich dark colors of the vegetable are heightened by the first thinned layer of transparent paint.

2

The second image demonstrates painting the edge from outside the form, or "cutting in." This is important in defining the characteristic head of the vegetable, and also for the distinctive smooth outlines.

3

Once the cutting in has been done, the pattern or texture of the surrounding cloth is restored with horizontal strokes, and this helps it recede again behind the eggplant, which should be the main focus of the image.

4

The full form is filled in with a colorful mid-tone, and into this wet paint a pale tint (not pure white but the appropriate tint) is dragged across the top of the paint, wet-on-wet, to create the shine of the smooth surface.

ORANGES (COLOR)

This example looks at the color relationships between the fruit and their warm shadows.

1

The oranges are quickly sketched in thinned oils, and brown shadows are laid in.

2

When the fruit are blocked in with more opaque paint, the texture requires some stippling, or dabbing of the brush, to create the pitted surface of these fruit.

3

The shiny white marks added now are made from very pale orange tints and are stippled with even more paint on the end of the brush to ensure that some remains unmixed and therefore stands out as the lightest. Sometimes this needs to be repeated a couple of times with fresh clean color.

4

Finally, the cream color of the sheet is developed with a blue-white mixture—the blue will help to balance the rich warm colors in the fruit with those in the surrounding areas and, being complementary, the orange subjects stand out all the more brightly.

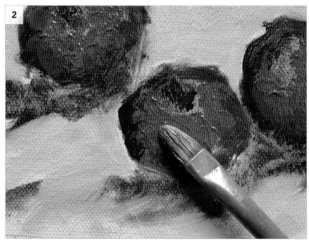

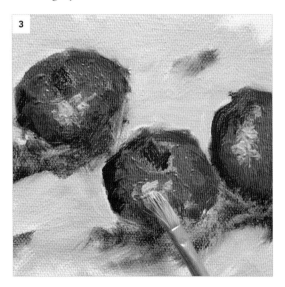

ONION (LAYERS)

Sometimes the *alla prima* oil painter needs to deconstruct their subject, rather like a sculptor might, in order to build it in paint. This, in turn, can require painting things in a certain order.

1

Effectively, the underlayers of the onion are the thinned underpainting, which is painted first. Darks are painted to full strength.

2

The thinly painted underlayers are fainter and recede beneath the outer layers of the vegetable, which are painted with thicker, more opaque marks.

3

The characteristic shedding of the onion's skin is suggested by the broken edges where the background colors meet the outside of the form, as well as where the underlayer shows through.

RENOIR & STILL LIFE
Masterclass: Bottle & Glass

STILL LIFE WITHIN A LARGER COMPOSITION

Many of Renoir's larger figure compositions of dances or friends eating and drinking together often contain a still life somewhere in the picture. It is likely that he worked on these elements separately from his models—perhaps while he was waiting for the next sitter, or for the paint to dry. It is also likely, knowing the spontaneous way that Renoir evolved his paintings, that the still life might have been superimposed onto a part of the composition. It will be worth working on these elements, practicing especially anything that is likely to appear in a larger composition.

1

A bottle and a glass are set up with a cloth behind to provide a background color, and an old painting is used for the canvas. Working on old paintings can be very satisfying as they often have textured surfaces, and the colors already present can contribute to the way you develop your new color scheme.

The new composition is roughly sketched out with diluted paint, and the background around the objects blocked in.

2

Fluid (but opaque) paint is used to sketch out some of the darker and mid-toned colors in the arrangement. The background is sketched in with plenty of gaps showing through to the old painting below. This helps integrate the still life into the larger composition, and helps the artist to do less in capturing the subject.

3

This particular pair of objects offer some of the challenges that Renoir seem to enjoy so much: colored liquid held inside reflective glass vessels, for example. Certain features are saved for later—notably the reflections and the strength of color in the liquid. The bottle and glass are partially defined by some gray lines and shapes, and partly by using the colors of the background in the vessels themselves as well as through the negative shapes around them.

4

The painting surface is wet with fairly thin paint, and this allows the ideal amount of blending of the new colors that are added, giving soft transitions from one color or tone to another. When a much stronger effect is required, such as the shining reflection on the bottle or the brighter color in the liquid, then the paint needs to be applied more thickly. More paint needs to be ready on the palette for this, and the brush technique involves dropping the paint as decisively as possible at the best point on the glass surface. This sort of emphasis cannot really be redone if you get it wrong the first time—it would probably be better to rub the whole passage out and have another try.

RENOIR & STILL LIFE
Exercise

1 STILL LIFE EXPERIMENTS

The aim of this exercise is to get you thinking more creatively about how you can apply paint. Don't worry too much about the resulting picture, just enjoy experimenting and think about how you might use these techniques in future paintings.

Set up a still life with objects that you know will be challenging to represent—pick things with interesting surfaces and textures (top).

Begin painting the objects in the two stages you're by now familiar with—thinned and then thicker paint—but do it without using brushes. Collect various implements such as cut pieces of mounting card, sponge, rollers, palette knives, cutlery, scrunched up paper, sticks and so on (bottom).

When it comes to selecting your implement, try to think about the result you're hoping to achieve. If you want to spread the paint out, don't choose a very small implement. But, on the other hand, also be prepared for unexpected results, and ready to grasp any happy accidents.

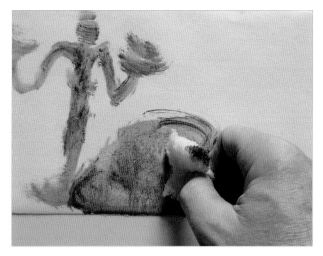 

Top left and right: Sponges are very good for drawing with the thinned paint at the initial stages, while printmakers' rollers are great for applying diluted paint in a highly textured way.

Bottom left and right: When you move to the stage of using thicker, more opaque paint, choose implements that can pick up the paint and deposit it onto the canvas surface. It can help if the paint is very slightly fluid, so that it is more easily picked up and then released from the implement, and deposited onto the picture. Also think about the kind of marks you want to make: a stick or the edge of a piece of mounting board will be ideal for linework, while the scrunched up piece of paper works perfectly to create the impression of flowers.

The value of this exercise is that it will make you more conscious of the consistency of the paint and of the variety of marks you can make as you depict the world you are painting. Brushwork can often feel repetitive and limited, but this experience will help you develop a richer variety in the ways in which you apply paint, and help you to do it more descriptively.

Develop your painting further if you want, and see how far you can go.

CHAPTER 7: RENOIR'S NUDES

A lover of the female form in general, Renoir celebrated the female nude as one of the greatest subjects for painting. He greatly admired Rubens and many of his nudes recall this Master's work. After his crisis of painting when he tried to be more rigorous with his drawing, and created quite rigid, outlined and "Ingriste" figures, he returned to the theme of the nude bather in the landscape with a new, warmer palette.

In these paintings Renoir demonstrates all the oil-painting techniques we have explored so far—thin dilute washes, thicker built-up impasto *taches* and transparent glazes. He described his particular aims in his rendering of flesh: "I must find the tints which will make the flesh on my canvas live and quiver."

Renoir's nudes tend to be in timeless and archetypal settings—young female bathers by the river or in the woods—and although they are rendered in the heightened colors of the Impressionist movement they are reminiscent of the painted nymphs and goddesses of earlier centuries.

Although for the sake of clarity I have described each of these techniques separately—and in the case of a more systematic artist, they probably would be used in a fairly systematic way—Renoir was a much more spontaneous creature. Notwithstanding technical considerations such as thick paint needing to be dry before glazing or scumbling can be applied on top, Renoir would probably have used all these different techniques simultaneously in different parts of the painting, depending on what was needed and, I suspect, what he could get away with. You will probably already have experienced some degree of scumbling or glazing on your canvas: whenever oil paint is mixed with linseed oil and turps its transparency is increased, so wherever this mixture is put down it will have a micro-glazing or scumbling effect on the layers beneath it. This chapter will look at the practical application of these effects in more detail.

RENOIR'S NUDES
Glazing

A glaze is a thin transparent layer that, when spread across a dry textured surface, will modify the appearance of the paint underneath, potentially making it darker, or more or less colorful. Glazing can't make the paint lighter, but it can make the layers underneath brighter in such a way that they appear to glow.

In this small study, a thinly painted start is followed by a thick impasto layer of warm skin colors (top right). In order for the next stage of glazing to really make an impact, the paint surface needs to be dry, and ideally it should be raised and textured in some way—the same will also be true of the scumbling technique.

The transparent glazed layer can be made by thinning the paint with linseed oil and turps, or other synthetic media that can be bought specifically for this purpose. You will want the paint to be extremely thin in order to create the subtle effect you are after.

Here, a warm glaze made from alizarin crimson, ultramarine and lemon yellow was spread across, wiped back and dabbed with a rag to modify the effect (bottom right and opposite). In this way it will cover both the thinner underpainting and the thick top layer, and it will bring these together creating subtle transitions that model the form and contours of the nude. It is particularly effective for creating subtle shadows and it can also create an enormous amount of depth. Like Rubens before him, Renoir often modeled the round and cylindrical forms of the body—the limbs, the torso—by painting dark edges and gradually lightening toward the center with thicker trails of paint creating the highlights.

RENOIR'S NUDES
Scumbling

Scumbling is a painting technique in which a small amount of opaque or semi-opaque paint is spread thinly and roughly over the dry and textured layers beneath in such a way that the layers beneath show through. This gives a translucent effect with plenty of depth. Scumbling can modify the paint below by making it darker, lighter or more or less colorful, but it cannot generate the luminous colors that glazing can.

In this example, a semi-opaque warm green mixture was made from chrome yellow, viridian and a touch of cadmium orange, and scumbled across the contours of the figure.

This layer covers parts of the thin first layer and also goes across the thicker impasto layer, thereby bringing them together and softening the transition from the more thickly applied highlights to the thinner dark paint that describes the contours of the body.

RENOIR'S NUDES
Alla Prima

Alla prima, or wet-on-wet handling of oil paint generates its own subtle transitions from color to color as the paint mixes on the surface of the canvas, which can be used to great effect.

The several stages of an *alla prima* study illustrated on these pages demonstrate painting in a certain order that involves laying in each lighter skin tone with a gradually smaller brush. These warm skin tones have been pre-mixed on the palette and, when applied to the canvas, they are pressed into the preceding layer of wet paint so that the edge of each new mark is softened, and a more subtle transition between colors is created.

In the far right image on the opposite page, a palette knife is being used to mix the colors a little more on the surface of the painting. A palette knife is a good tool for this step because it will remove less paint from the surface than your brush is likely to. It is also a lot easier to clean—wiping it on old newspaper or telephone books will do the trick—so you won't unintentionally be adding pigment where you don't want it. The palette knife acts a bit like an Impressionist's fan brush—slightly and roughly mixing color, half scraping it down into the canvas at the same time, but with a loose control over the whole process.

RENOIR'S NUDES
Masterclass: Bathing Nude

PAINTING FLESH

The twentieth-century American artist Willem de Kooning famously said that "flesh was the reason that oil paint was invented," and artists through the ages have used a variety of ways of handling oil paint in order to render skin convincingly. One generally tends to think of skin as a smooth surface, and painters of the distant past might have used a fan brush to smoothly blend one skin color or tone with the next, so that the transition was almost invisible. The Impressionists, however, seeking to heighten color and intensify the effect of their paintings, worked instead with an effect called "optical mixing." This is the effect you can observe when you stand back from one of Renoir's Impressionist paintings, and all his colorful *taches* blend

in the eye. Transitions are created, but the contrasts between the colors remain vibrant. For the fullest effect the Impressionists often placed complementary colors side by side, such as pinks and greens. From a distance the hues appear natural, but they are in fact very colorful.

If you want to blend one skin tone into another without resorting to the fan brush, and if you also don't want to have to mix the "one thousand tints" that Renoir said he saw when he considered his subject, then subtle transitions from one color to another can be made by glazing, scumbling and working *alla prima*. This Masterclass demonstrates how all the techniques we have looked at can be used together to depict flesh—the apogee of painterly subjects.

1

The painting begins with a loose thin sketch reminiscent of a watercolor painting. The warm colors of the flesh overlap and mix with the cool colors of the water behind the bather, and the resulting mixtures generate soft edges.

2

A warm red-brown line is then run along the edges of the arms and legs, imparting a luminous heat to the figure. As mentioned, this is quite a traditional way of rendering skin; the cylindrical forms of limbs and torsos outlined with a warm mid-tone. This warmth is also used as an undercoat for the figure's hair—even black hair (which Renoir celebrated in his many paintings of Gabrielle, his wife's cousin and a favorite model) needs to be warmed in order that it should harmonize with the rest of the body.

Lighter and thicker trails of paint are dragged across parts of the body in directions that follow the form of the figure. Thicker, paler grays are added to the towel. These highlights will stand out both because of their tonal lightness and also because the paint is more substantial in these places.

3

At this stage the balance between temperatures is re-established, as cool marks are applied to the rocks, water and hair. Some of the greens in the rocks are also applied to parts of the figure, creating cooler skin colors in the shadows.

4

In this next stage of the nude, a dark green glaze is used to emphasize some of the shadow areas and darker edges of the figure. Ideally, a glaze should be made from transparent pigments (you can look up a chart of the properties of particular pigments to find out which are transparent, or semi-transparent—I used viridian (transparent) and cadmium orange (semi-transparent), which gave me a sufficiently transparent, or translucent product when mixed with a medium (such as Liquin) to make the subtle modulations to the skin colors in my nude. The subtle changes are created by controlling the strength of the glaze. When I spread it thinly it hardly darkens the marks underneath, but applied in a slightly stronger way it will have a significant impact on the tonal value of the marks beneath it. Significantly, the advantage of the glaze or the scumble is that generally they retain the texture and variety of the marks over which they are laid.

5

Now more brush marks, or taches *of pale warm skin tones are applied with smaller brush. This needs to be a stiff hog hair brush—a soft brush won't be able to pick up and deposit the quantities needed at this stage. These marks are mixed a little by scraping and scratching with a palette knife in the directions of the contours of the figure. Some swatches of the colors used are illustrated. A glaze-like yellow-brown mixture is also spread over the water in order to add contrast and depth to this area. It is a good way of capturing the complexity of water, the surface of which is at once transparent and reflective. A scumble of yellows is applied over the rocks. The significant point to make about these techniques is that Renoir liked to use glazing and scumbling because they create very subtle variations in color and tone, as well as making it possible to maintain the gaps in the painted surface through to the luminous colors beneath.*

6

A detail of the white towel, the folds of which are emphasized by using thicker white brush marks. These can be softened with thinner paint if they seem to stand out too much.

7

The painting is left to dry for a day or two. It is important when returning to a painting after a break to maintain an awareness of the whole composition—to continue to work on different areas and bring them along together. Sometimes it can be helpful to bring out strong contrast in certain parts of the picture, so that other contrasts of color and tone can be compared with the brightest color or lightest tone.

Here, the colors in the water, rocks and towel are heightened to create a standard against which the intensity of color and tone in the skin can be measured. The process of applying taches *continues, and a quick glaze-like layer is applied to redefine the hair and the outlines of the limbs. Small warm skin marks are built up using a small dry brush and overlapping each color with the next to allow some blending of the color and tone. Some pale colors as well as some warm and colorful shades are needed in mid-tone areas (including the middle areas of the limbs and torso). Then the shadow colors are advanced with green and yellow marks.*

8

In the final stages of the painting, more dry brush marks are used to build up all the different skin colors—pinks, yellows, oranges, and blues and greens in the shadows. The overlapping short marks begin to combine to make a good balance of both muted and vibrant skin tones. A very light pale orange is mixed as a balance to the lightest white marks in the towel. As ever, at the same time as developing colors in the nude, it is necessary to heighten some of the surrounding sets of colors, such as the water, which up to this point has been mainly warm bright blues. Now, some cooler green-blues are added to increase the contrast of color. Lighter, brighter yellows are added to the rocks for a similar effect.

RENOIR'S NUDES
Exercises

1 PAINTING NUDES

Pose your model, but pre-mix your colors and make up or borrow a background from another painting or photograph, so that the only complexity you're dealing with is the flesh tones and how to render them in a naturalistic, but heightened way. It is far better to work from life if you can, but if you are working from a photograph for the figure, then make sure it is well lit so that you can get the best possible impression of the qualities of the flesh.

Begin a small painting of a nude using some cool, diluted blues or greens in the background, and warm skin colors (top left). The edges of the figure should be allowed to mix to create some neutrals for softer transitions.

Mix the colors you see on your canvas in thicker paint (top center). Aim to mix a palette where Renoir's "one thousand tiny tints" have been reduced to about five or six warm skin tones, plus pairs of colors (middle and lighter tones) for the background areas.

Now try applying them using the short decisive brush mark, or *tache* (top right). This can feel counterintuitive, but if you are patient and stand back a lot from the painting, the colors will begin to work together. Try holding the very end of the long brush handle, and even looking at the painting with your eyes half closed. This will help you to experience the optical mixing more readily and make you less likely to smooth out the differences in color and tone.

Once the background and figure have been treated with this first set of colors, it is likely that the skin will look too crude and will need more subtle colors to bridge the existing set (bottom right). Rather than blend what is there, try to mix a new set that you will apply in between the marks already made. Adding white alone will not be enough; you need to look at the skin colors as varieties of pink, orange and yellow— lighter and mid-tone as well as colorful and muted. Build up a few marks, still avoiding letting them blend, and then develop the background range—perhaps one more lighter tone for each area.

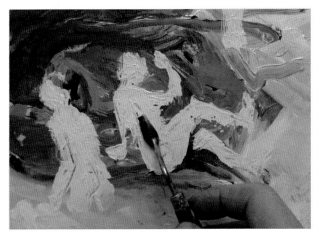

2 TECHINIQUES FOR NUDES

Paint a series of nude figures (borrowed from Renoir, if you wish) using a warm pink mixture of acrylic paint, blocked in with a palette knife (top left). If you do this on an old painting—particularly one with some dark areas—some definition can be achieved by scraping into the background. The aim is to prepare some areas of flesh that can be modeled through later stages of glazing and scumbling.

Prepare a warm dark glaze from a mixture of alizarin crimson, ultramarine and lemon yellow, thinned with linseed oil and turps. Apply this to create shadow areas on one of the acrylic figures, applying it more intensely for darks, and faintly for weaker shadows (top right).

Also mix a cool scumble from cobalt blue, viridian and white, again thinned with oil and spirit. Try this technique out on a different figure (bottom left).

With both your scumbles and your glazes, experiment with slightly reducing the effect by lifting off some glaze or scumble with a clean rag (bottom right). Add and subtract until you feel you have achieved the most subtle range possible. Let the glaze and the scumble dry before adding further layers of opaque color and tone—always endeavoring not to obliterate the delicate effects of these approaches.

GLOSSARY

alla prima
Italian term literally meaning "at the first attempt." Oil-painting technique where canvas is completed in one session before the paint has dried, in contrast to the slower method of building the painting up one layer at a time. Also known as "wet-on-wet" and "direct painting."

atelier
Artist's workshop or studio.

canvas
Fabric surface for painting on. Can also refer to the completed oil painting.

charcoal
Carbon-based drawing sticks made from wood (usually willow) burnt without air, available in various different sizes and degrees of hardness.

complementary
One of a pair of colors situated opposite each other on a color wheel—for example, green is the complementary color of red.

composition
The design or arrangement of the different parts of a drawing or painting.

crop
To cut off or mask unwanted areas.

en plein air
Painting conducted "in the open air," or out of doors, rather than in the studio.

float
To lay oil paint lightly on the (wet) surface of a painting.

gesso
Plaster mixed with glue to seal canvas or other surfaces onto which oil paint is to be applied, to prevent oil soaking through.

glaze
Thin, transparent layer of paint.

gouache
Water-based paint in which pigment is bound with gum.

ground
The surface onto which paint is applied, usually first coated with a primer, such as gesso.

impasto
Painting technique where paint is applied thickly, so that it stands out from the surface of the canvas.

Impressionism
Style of painting developed towards the end of the nineteenth century, characterized by short brush strokes, heightened colors and an interest in the effects of daylight. Canvases were often painted *en plein air* and reflected the everyday lives of working people, as opposed to the highly stylised, studio-based works conventional at the time.

ingriste
Following the style of Ingres; a disciple of Ingres.

juice
Renoir's name for the paint diluted with turpentine and linseed oil to a transparent and highly fluid consistency with which he liked to begin his paintings.

linseed oil
Paint binder commonly found in oil paints, also used as a paint medium to make oils more fluid and transparent.

master
A senior artist under whom an apprentice or student of art would train.

medium
1. The material or materials used to create a work of art, such as pastel or oil paint.
2. Substance added to paints to control and alter their consistency.

mounting board
Cardboard onto which prints are mounted for display. Off-cuts are useful mark-making implements when working with the monotype technique.

oil paint
Pigment ground in oil; usually linseed oil.

Old Masters
Collective term for certain European artists working before 1800, whose work was characterized by great technical skill and beauty.

opaque/opacity
An opaque pigment, when applied, will conceal the layer beneath it. Oil paints vary in opacity, with the level usually indicated on the label of the pigment. Titanium white is an example of a highly opaque pigment.

palette
1. Smooth surface on which paints can be mixed in preparation for painting.
2. The set or range of colors used by a particular artist or in a particular work.

pigment
A coloring matter or substance, such as oil paint or pastel.

scumble
To soften the color of a painted area by overlaying with opaque color applied thinly with an almost dry brush.

stipple
To paint with dots or small spots.

tone (or value)
Lightness or darkness of a color or mark, independent of its hue.

tooth
Rough surface of paper or pastel-coated paper that has been sprayed with fixative.

translucent/translucency
Semi-transparent or partially opaque paint that lets some detail of the layer beneath come through.

transparent/transparency
A pigment that, when applied, still shows the layer beneath it. The amount of transparency will vary according to how thickly the paint is applied, as well as the transparency of the pigment itself, which is usually indicated on the label.

turpentine (turps)
A solvent distilled from resin, used for the thinning of oil-based paints.

underpainting
The first layers of a painting, often used to establish the basic design, tones or color scheme of the developed painting.

value
See tone.

wet-on-wet
See alla prima.

INDEX

alizarin crimson 12, 66–67, 85, 94–95, 98, 110, 121
alla prima 7, 25, 35, 40–41, 48, 51, 57, 59–60, 64, 75, 89, 93, 100–103, 114–16
Arran from Skipness 37, 42–43
Auerbach, Frank 32

back to front 82
background 13, 84–85, 90–91, 99, 105, 120–21
Bather and Maid 32, 33
The Bathers 32
Bathing Nude 116–19
board 18–19
Bottle & Glass 104–5
Boucher, Francois 21
Bouquet of Chrysanthemums 31
brush techniques 56–59
brushes 13, 45, 51, 106
butter-style palette knives 13

cadmium orange 63, 112, 117
canvas 12–13, 18–19, 39, 41–42, 94
catchlights 68
charcoal 37, 48, 52
Charpentier, Madame 27, 55
chins 71
chrome yellow 12, 38, 50, 63, 98–99, 112
Claude Lorrain 25
close up 20–33
clouds 49, 53
cobalt blue 12, 38, 40–41, 50, 67, 87, 94–95, 121
color 98–99, 102, 116
color temperature 64–67, 99, 117
color theory 22
color wheel 64
commissions 27, 55

composition 18–19, 36–39, 41, 44, 52, 79–83, 104–5, 118
consistency of paint 60–63, 96, 107
Constable, John 39
contre jour 36, 88
cool colors 64–67, 99, 116, 119–20
cutting in 101

Daffodils & View Through Trees 48–51
Dance at Le Moulin de la Galette 28
Dappled Light 86–89
de Kooning, Willem 32, 116
Degas, Edgar 7
depth 36, 45, 59, 67, 74, 81–82, 88, 91, 98, 110, 112
descriptive marks 57
detail 45, 48, 51, 59, 72–75, 80, 84–87, 90
developing paintings 40–41
displaying work 15–16
double dippers 13, 19
draftsmanship 21
drawing 17–18, 83

easels 14, 18
eggplants 101
emphasis 48–49, 63, 75, 85, 90, 105
equipment 14–15
etchings 17
exercises 8, 11, 49–53, 76–77, 90–91, 106–7, 120–21
experiments 106–7
eyes 13, 68

faces 13, 55
features 13, 55, 68–71, 77
figure groups 26–29, 78–91
flake white 12

flesh 32, 60, 109, 116–20
flowers 17, 93–94, 96–97, 107
Flowers in a Vase 96–97
folding easels 18
foreshortening 68–69
Formica 14, 19
Fragonard, Jean 21
framing 36–37, 52
Freud, Lucian 32
Fruits of the Midi 93

gesso 65
ghost figures 80
Girl Reading in Window Seat 60–63
Girls at the Piano 26–27
glass palettes 14
glazing 7, 57, 62–64, 66–67, 75, 95, 109–12, 116–18, 121
Gleyre, Charles 7, 25

hair 55
handling paint 60–63, 96–97, 100, 114
happy accidents 7, 35, 98, 106
heaters 16
highlights 48, 56, 110, 112, 117
hog hair brushes 13, 45, 51, 56–57, 62, 96, 118
horizon 36–37, 52, 82, 91
house-painting brushes 13

impasto 7, 13, 25, 57, 97, 109–10, 112
Impressionists 7–8, 13, 16–17, 19, 21–22, 25, 27–28, 32–33, 35, 37, 44–45, 49, 52, 55, 79, 83, 86, 89, 93, 95, 109, 114, 116
individual features 68–71

Ingriste figures 109
ivory black 12

juices 38, 41–42, 56, 60, 72, 80, 86, 94, 100

Kooning, Willem de 32, 116

landscapes 22–24
larger composition 104–5
layers 7, 47, 53, 64, 72, 77, 80, 94, 96–99, 103, 109–10, 112
lemon yellow 65–67, 110, 121
life drawing 16–17
lighting 16
line drawing 17, 52
linseed oil 13, 19, 22, 50, 56, 68, 72, 87, 94–95, 109–10, 121
Liquin 117
long-handled brushes 13
Louvre 21
luminosity 98
Luncheon of the Boating Party 28–29, 80, 83

Madame Charpentier 27, 55
madder red 12
Manet, Édouard 7, 21
masterclasses 8, 11, 42–43, 48–51, 60–67, 72–75, 79–80, 84–89, 96–99, 104–5, 116–19
materials 12–13
mediums 19
Meloncillo brushes 13
models 16–17, 32, 55, 60, 76–77, 90–91, 104, 117, 120
Monet, Claude 7, 11, 21–22, 35, 55
mouths 13, 69

Museé d'Orsay 7
Museé du Luxembourg 27

Naples yellow 12, 41, 98
near & far at once 80–81
noses 70–71
Nude in Sunlight 32
nudes 16, 32–33, 108–21

Oarsmen at Chatou 28
ocher 12, 50, 73
offcuts 94
oil paint 7–8, 12–13, 15, 17,
    19, 21, 32, 35, 44, 56,
    58–63, 75, 89, 116
oil/turps/media 13, 19, 50,
    56, 68, 72, 87, 94–95,
    109–10, 121
Old Masters 7, 21–22, 63,
    109
onions 103
optical mixing 116, 120
oranges 102
organic development 91

palette knives 13, 40, 106,
    114, 118, 121
palettes 14, 19, 40, 48, 93, 98,
    109, 114
Peaches on a Plate 30
pencil drawings 83
perspective 36–37, 52,
    79–80, 82, 91
photographs 17, 28, 53, 80,
    90–91, 120
en plein air 11, 15, 17–19, 22,
    25, 34–53, 55–56, 79, 86,
    100
poppy-seed oil 13
Portrait of a Boy 64–67
Portrait of a Girl 72–75
portraits 26–29, 54–77
poses 16
Poussin, Nicolas 25

prints 17
props 16

Raphael 21
raw sienna 12
Reclining Odalisque 32
rivers 47, 52
rollers 106–7
Rubens, Peter Paul 21, 32,
    63, 109–10

sable brushes 51, 56, 61, 68,
    73
scale 52, 79, 91
scumbling 7, 32, 57, 62, 64,
    74–75, 95, 109–10,
    112–13, 116–18, 121
selecting compositions
    36–37
self-portraits 76
shadows 38, 44, 47, 71, 74–5,
    87–9, 91, 98, 110, 117–19,
    121
sheep 46
silhouettes 41, 88
Sisley, Alfred 7
sketches 17–18, 36–38, 48,
    52, 77, 83, 90
skies 41, 49–51, 53, 81–82
slices of life 28
soft brushes 13
sponges 106–7
spotlights 16
starting compositions 38–39
stiff-haired brushes 13
still life 17, 30–31, 92–107
studio set-up 10–19
studio space 15
subject matter 16–17
surfaces 39
swatches 94

taches 7, 22, 44–45, 86, 89,
    95, 109, 116, 118, 120

texture 101, 104, 106, 110,
    117
Titian 32
tracing paper 83
transport 18–19
trees 45, 49–53, 91
trowel-style palette knives 13
tubes 19, 22
turpentine 13, 19, 50, 56, 68,
    72, 87, 94–95, 109–10, 121
Two Girls in the Garden
    84–85

ultramarine 12, 65–67, 110,
    121
umber 50
underdrawing 65, 83
underpainting 32, 44, 47, 96,
    103, 110

vermillion 12
Veronese green 12
viewfinders 17, 19, 36
viewpoints 18, 70, 77
viridian 12, 38, 50, 63, 85,
    98–99, 112, 117, 121

warm colors 64–67, 99, 102,
    109–10, 112, 114, 116–21
watercolors 56
The Watering Place 24–25
weather 18
wet-on-wet 7, 35, 89, 101,
    114
*Woman with a Parasol
    in a Garden* 22–23, 25
wooden palettes 14
working order 41
workspace 14–15
worn brushes 45

Yellow Roses 98–99

ACKNOWLEDGMENTS

I need to thank Pierre-Auguste Renoir for being the reason for writing this book and for having taught me so much, particularly about color and paint handling. I also owe a debt to Bernard Dunstan R.A. for his analysis and clear explanations of Renoir's methods. I would like to thank Luke Ker for finding me the right book at the right time and my painting students for trying things out and then demonstrating to me just how well they can work.

Above all, I want to thank Ruth, Isaac, Iris, Inez and Yvan for patiently believing in my efforts.

Finally, thanks again to the Ilex team—Zara for asking, Nick, Natalia and Rachel for guiding me through, and Julie for the excellent design.

PICTURE CREDITS